Woodfinishing
Handbook

D0068025

Woodfinishing Handbook

IAN HOSKER

GUILD OF MASTER CRAFTSMAN PUBLICATIONS LTD

First published 1995 by Guild of Master
Craftsman Publications Ltd 166 High Street
Lewes East Sussex BN7 1XU

© Ian Hosker 1993, 1995

ISBN 0 946819 70 X

Illustrations Tim Benké 1993
Photographs © Ian Hosker 1993, 1995,
except where otherwise credited.
Cover photograph by David Maxwell
All rights reserved
This edition is a revised and condensed
version of *Complete Woodfinishing*, published in
1993 by Guild of Master Craftsman
Publications Ltd

Designed by Ian Hunt Design

Typeface: Meridien
Printed and bound in Singapore under the
supervision of MRM Graphics, Winslow,
Bucks, UK.

To Barbara,
Samantha and David

CONTENTS

ACKNOWLEDGEMENTS

This book is the result of my experiences of teaching furniture restoration and woodfinishing over a number of years. It grew out of the many requests I have received for information which is sufficiently detailed to be worth the effort of reading, but which is not so technical as to be difficult to use.

Therefore, I am grateful to those students, who, through their requests for clear, detailed and concise information on the craft, provided me with the framework which forms the basis of this book. I am also indebted to my family, who have patiently tolerated my many hours of absence, and to whom this book is dedicated.

INTRODUCTION

The aim of this book is to help you create a good colour and polish on any wood product, whether it be your front door, the built-in furniture or the mahogany table you bought at the local auction which you now feel was a mistake!

For some reason, there has been an air of mystique surrounding woodfinishing for an extremely long time. Oddly, this has not been helped in recent years by the almost explosive growth of products that claim to make the task easier! In fact, the wealth of choice available may serve only to confuse. I hope

this book will go a long way to remove the cloud of confusion, and present a logical explanation of the materials and processes used to decorate and protect wood.

None of the methods of woodfinishing described is too difficult to master, or requires a special talent possessed only by a few. It is all a matter of practice and confidence – the former developing the latter.

Whatever your woodfinishing needs, I hope that you find this book a useful reference source which will help you to produce satisfying results.

1
CHOOSING THE RIGHT FINISH

- To enhance the natural beauty of wood's grain texture and surface markings (referred to as 'figure').
- To produce an even colour and surface that is pleasing to look at and which fits in well with the surroundings.
- To protect the wood from a wide variety of things that will destroy, damage or disfigure it in some way.

Many a good piece of craftsmanship has been ruined by poor staining and polishing. While not everyone can French polish there are alternatives that can make a piece look just as good, and there is no real excuse for 'bodging'. Bodged jobs arise for two main reasons:

- Lack of knowledge, skill and experience of the wide range of finishing materials that are now available to both professional and amateur.
- Lack of *planning*. Finishing is often left out of the 'thinking it through' process; consequently very little attention is given to it.

Planning is a matter of good working practice. Before you touch the first piece of wood to start your project, you should already know what its final surface will look like because you will have asked yourself a number of questions which will set the criteria for choosing a finish.

For example:

- Will it have to be a particular colour?
- Will it be handled a great deal?
- Will it be subjected to possible water or alcohol spillages?
- Will it look better with a high gloss, low lustre or totally matt finish?
- Will it be indoors or out?
- Will the nature of the wood itself determine the best method of finishing (e.g. is there an attractive figure that needs to be brought out; is the wood likely to reject certain finishes)?
- Is there a traditional way of finishing this particular wood?
- Does the piece have to match other items?
- What skills do I have?

THE WRONG FINISH

There can be unfortunate and disappointing consequences if:

- The wrong type of finish is applied.
- The type of stain is incompatible with the polish material or solvent.
- Incorrect surface preparation has taken place.

Fig 1.1 shows an exterior door with the varnish peeling off and bad staining due to moisture. Normal internal polyurethane varnish is unsuitable because the constant movement of the door, expanding and contracting as atmospheric conditions change, causes such varnish to crack due to its inflexibility. This in turn allows water to penetrate and lift the varnish.

Alternatively, it could be that moisture was trapped in the wood prior to finishing, or that the stain used was not quite dry. The result would be the same, and one of the new breed of microporous varnishes would have been better (see Chapter 7).

Fig 1.2 shows the badly ring-marked surface of a French polished table. This very beautiful but vulnerable finish is not resistant to heat, alcohol or moisture. Perhaps in this case a burnished polyurethane varnish might have been more suitable (see Chapter 7).

Fig 1.1 The varnish on this exterior door has broken down, resulting in rainwater penetration.

Fig 1.2 French polish is vulnerable to moisture, heat, alcohol and other solvents. Here, a white ring mark can be clearly seen on a French polished surface; such marks are most commonly caused by moisture on the bottom of cups or glasses, or hot objects.

Towards the end of this chapter is a flowchart (Table 1) which will help you decide upon the best finish for the job. By answering the questions you will be led step by step to a finish that should fit the bill. The chart will also direct you to the appropriate sections of the book where you can read up on your chosen finish.

Chapters 3 and 4 are essential reading, as the procedures are the same no matter what you plan to do, and Chapter 4 contains some information on certain stains which are potentially incompatible with the final polish, and should be checked before continuing. It goes

without saying that Chapter 11 on health and safety should be regarded as obligatory.

Finally, at the end of this book, Chapter 12 is devoted to recipes for making polishes, cleaners and revivers, and a number of other useful substances that the woodfinisher may need, and which can be successfully made at home, in small or large amounts.

TRADITIONAL FINISHING

Just because something is done traditionally does not, of course, bind you to doing the same, but it should at least influence your eventual choice of finish for different woods. After all, traditions are based on what experience has shown to work.

Oak, pine and teak seem to please the eye more when they are finished to a low lustre (see Fig 1.3). Oak was traditionally waxed, oiled or simply burnished. Its coarse grain texture and medullary ray figuring (on quarter-sawn boards) are certainly shown off at their best if the grain is left open (i.e. no grain filler has been used) and there is no high build-up of polish. This creates the impression that you are touching the wood itself when you run your fingers over it, as most people are tempted to do.

Pine is a curious one, in that it was not used as a decorative wood in its own right during the eighteenth and nineteenth centuries. Pine furniture was usually utilitarian in nature, being relegated to the servants' areas and the kitchen. It would frequently be quite bare, with kitchen tables usually being scrubbed down each day with very hot water. At the other end of the social spectrum, pine furniture was frequently painted, often spectacularly so, and was chosen for this purpose for obvious reasons in preference to more expensive woods.

Walnut, mahogany and rosewood look superb under carefully applied French polish, where the optical qualities seem to enhance the attractive and dramatic figures characteristic of these timbers.

CHOOSING A FINISH

Table 1 can be used as a general guide to an appropriate finish for the job in hand. However, there may be other overriding factors to take into account.

Starting at the top, follow the arrows that give the appropriate criteria. For example, if the surface needs to be durable, you are led to the questions 'internal?' or 'external?'. Assuming the work is external, is it liable to be absorbing a lot of moisture or do you suspect that moisture may be present already? If the answer is yes, do you want a hard finish or a non-coating finish? Hard finish leads you to use microporous materials, and non-coating leads to solvent or oil-based preservative.

If, when you turn to the appropriate chapters, the finish is not exactly what you are looking for, you should seek an alternative, but you may need to compromise on specifications. For example, you may decide on French polish and therefore compromise on heat and water resistance.

Fig 1.3 The low lustre of pine suits its 'rustic' appearance. Waxing, or even oiling, will achieve this effect. However, this door has been finished with two coats of matt polyurethane because it is subject to a great deal of wear and tear. Overall, the effect is very much the same.

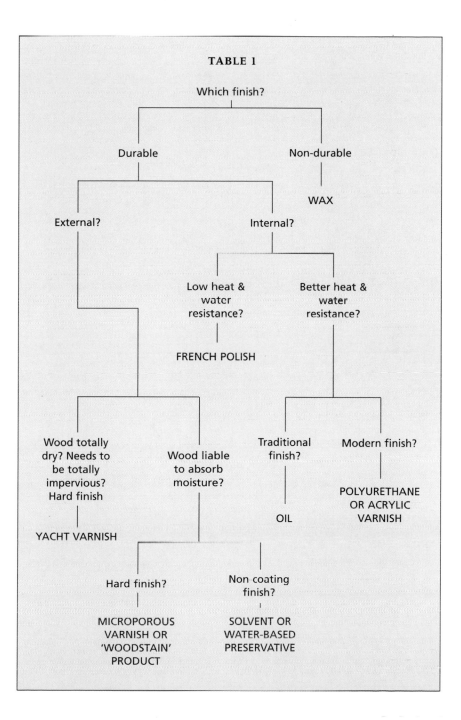

TABLE 1

Which finish?

Durable — Non-durable

WAX

External? — Internal?

Low heat &
water
resistance? — Better heat &
water
resistance?

FRENCH POLISH

Wood totally
dry? Needs to
be totally
impervious?
Hard finish — Wood liable
to absorb
moisture? — Traditional
finish? — Modern finish?

POLYURETHANE
OR ACRYLIC
VARNISH

OIL

YACHT VARNISH

Hard finish? — Non coating
finish?

MICROPOROUS
VARNISH OR
'WOODSTAIN'
PRODUCT — SOLVENT OR
WATER-BASED
PRESERVATIVE

METHOD OF WORKING

Always plan. Be meticulous in your approach to the work and, above all, do not rush things. If a varnish requires six hours to dry sufficiently to apply another coat, then leave it for six hours. This may seem patronizing, but believe me, the temptation to press on with the job can sometimes be overwhelming!

In general your order of working should be as follows:

▌ Prepare surface by filling or repairing blemishes, and smoothing.
▌ Stain (if required).
▌ Fill the grain (if required).
▌ Apply initial coat of polish.
▌ Correct any colour errors (if appropriate).
▌ Apply finishing coats of polish.

It is usual (except in the case of waxing and oiling) to gently rub down the surface between coats, partly to remove adhering particles but also to provide a key for the subsequent coat.

COMPATIBILITY

The issue of compatibility is extremely important. There are some materials that ought not to be used together because, for one reason or another, they will not *work* together. For example, French polish used over wax will not form a secure bond, and may begin to flake off as a result. Also, if a wood dye is not allowed sufficient time to dry before the application of polyurethane varnish, the colour may 'bleed' into the varnish, creating a patchy effect. A similar effect can occur if the wood is oiled too soon after staining.

Residue can also be a problem. After stripping an old finish and attempting to stain the surface a different colour, some of the old finish which has resisted the stripper may remain in the pores of the wood. This will prevent the stain from penetrating and leave unsightly light areas. The same thing may result from not having given the stripper enough time to work. Another effect occurs if the stripper has not been properly neutralized. Occasionally, when the new finish (such as French polish or polyurethane) is applied, it remains sticky because the remaining stripper prevents it from hardening.

All these problems can be avoided by following the procedures described in this book. There is always a tendency to desire rapid results, but it is very important to leave the correct time between processes. Sometimes the time lapse is precautionary, sometimes essential, but it is always there for a reason.

2
POWER SANDING

Power sanding is used at two stages of the finishing process:

- To produce a very smooth surface on the bare 'substrate' (the term for any surface to which a finish is applied) prior to staining and polishing.
- To cut back intermediate coats of polish.

There are three main types of sanding machines: disc, belt and orbital. Because the process of sanding is based on scratching away the surface with an abrasive material, the abrasive will leave its own marks. It is important that the abrasion takes place along the grain, otherwise there will be marks that show through the final finish, no matter how careful you have been (see Chapter 3).

DISC SANDER

This tool has no place in fine woodfinishing. It is a rough tool designed for indiscriminate removal of material without any regard for the quality of the final surface. Fig 2.1 shows the murderous effect of a disc sander on a flat substrate. As the disc rotates it cuts deeply across

the grain no matter how the abrasive is presented to the substrate. Such damage is virtually impossible to repair satisfactorily. Using a fine grade of abrasive will not help, as any cutting across the grain will always show through the final finish, especially if it is gloss.

Disc sanders must never be used on veneered work, as their action is so rapid and severe you will cut through to the substrate before there is any time to reverse the action.

BELT SANDER

As the name implies, these sanders have a belt of abrasive which runs over two rollers, with the working face running over a smooth metal base plate which presses the belt on to the substrate. Hand-held belt sanders (see Fig 2.2) are very useful for the initial preparation prior to hand sanding or using an orbital sander. They are designed to remove material rapidly and are frequently used to prepare the surface after it has been planed. As you will see in Chapter 3, machine planing does not produce a satisfactory surface and belt sanding is a really good way of quickly smoothing out the

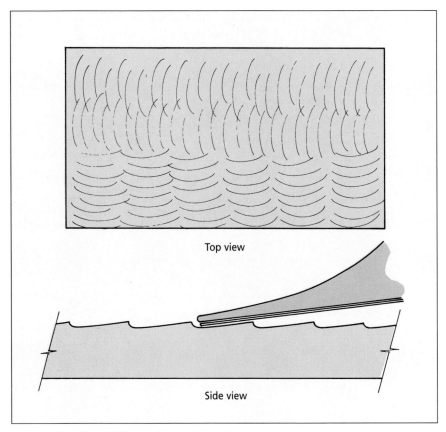

Top view

Side view

Fig 2.1 The effect of disc sanders on the surface of wood.

blemishes. However, belt sanders are not suitable for use on a veneered surface as, once again, they remove the wood too rapidly.

IN USE

As you push the machine along the wood (do not press down; the machine's own weight will be enough to create the right finish – just guide), the area of the belt in contact with the substrate opposes the movement of the tool. This has two advantages: first, friction, and consequently cutting action, is increased, and second, you have better control.

Despite the general advice of not using abrasive material against the grain, the belt sander does work better if it is allowed to cut at a slight angle to the grain direction (see Fig 2.3).

Fig 2.2 Hand-held belt sander with sanding frame.

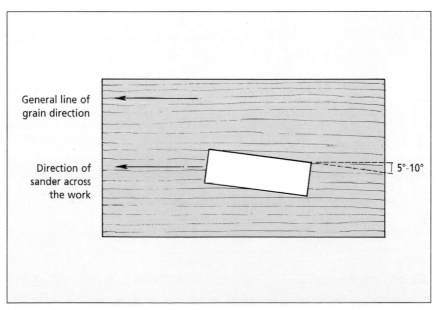

General line of
grain direction

Direction of
sander across
the work

5°-10°

Fig 2.3 Belt sanders should be presented at a slight angle to the general direction of the grain.

FEATURES TO LOOK FOR

The features to look for on a belt sander are the width of the belt, the speed, and the power of the motor. Belt widths range from 2in (51mm) on DIY models to about 4in (102mm) on professional hand-held machines. The average length of the sanding area is about 6in (152mm). The width and speed also determine the power of motor needed to drive the sander. The wider the belt, the greater the area in contact with the substrate and the greater the frictional force, requiring a more powerful motor to drive the belt smoothly at a good speed. However, the weight of the machine also increases with its belt and motor size, and a good compromise is a machine with a 3in (76mm) belt.

Belt speeds vary from about 300 metres to 500 metres per minute. Variable speed is a useful controlling device but is not essential on a belt sander and can be regarded as a luxury.

The depth of cut can be controlled with an adjustable sanding frame (shown in Figs 2.2 and 2.6) fixed to the base of the sander. This also increases the overall area of the base, helping to maintain a flat surface.

ORBITAL SANDER

Final sanding is achieved either by hand or using an orbital sander. This is a smoothing tool, not designed to remove large amounts of material. Consequently it should always be used with fine grades of abrasive paper.

Orbital sanders operate by rotating their base around a fixed position (hence the term orbital) so that each grain of abrasive rotates in a circle over the substrate, effectively scouring the surface. This is done at very high speed and the diameter of rotation is very small (see Fig 2.4). An orbital sander used with coarse paper grades would produce a large number of tiny circular scratches which would be very hard to remedy later.

IN USE

During use, orbital sanders can be moved over the whole surface in any direction, as the rotation of the base makes the rule of moving along the grain redundant. Do not use excessive pressure, as this will create poor surface quality, as well as being bad for the motor and reducing the life of the tool. As with the belt sander, the machine's own weight should be sufficient.

Used with fine grades of abrasive the action of an orbital sander is

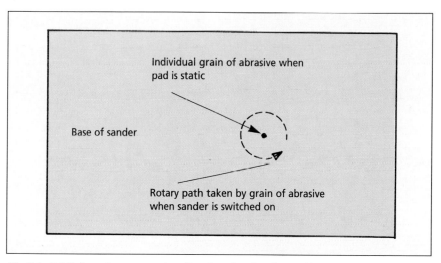

Individual grain of abrasive when pad is static

Base of sander

Rotary path taken by grain of abrasive when sander is switched on

Fig 2.4 Orbital sanders operate by vibrating the abrasive pad in a small circular path at very high speed.

very gentle and can be used with some confidence on veneered work. However, you should still take great care when refinishing pieces as the veneer is liable to be very thin. Orbital sanders can also be used to denib (remove dust specks) between coats of varnish or lacquer (but *not* French polish!).

FEATURES TO LOOK FOR

The faster the speed of the orbital action, the finer the finish. Again, speed controls are available on some models but are not normally required. The average orbital speed is around 4000–5000 orbits per minute, but more expensive machine speeds can run into five figures.

Orbital sanders are sized according to the area of the sanding base, and come in three basic sizes: third sheet, half sheet and quarter sheet. These refer to the proportion of a standard sheet of abrasive paper 11in x 9in (279mm x 229mm) which can be fitted. A half sheet machine is the best choice for most purposes, while the quarter sheet models are known as palm sanders. These fit snugly into the palm of the hand and are very useful for small, awkward areas like the insides of drawers (see Fig 2.5).

CHOOSING SANDERS

As a general rule, always buy the best tools and equipment you can afford. If you intend to do a lot of work it always pays to invest in quality. Nowadays the price of power tools is coming down while the quality of the machines is improving, mainly due to improvements in technology, manufacturing techniques and materials. Modern sanders tend to be lighter in weight, and are often better powered making them less fatiguing and more convenient to use as well as kinder on the pocket.

SAFE SANDING

A sanding machine should be switched on *before* being presented to the wood. Starting it up while in contact with the surface will create a dangerous torque which can wrench the machine from your grip and cause you or someone nearby an injury. The machine should be lifted from the surface before being switched off. Most machines have a

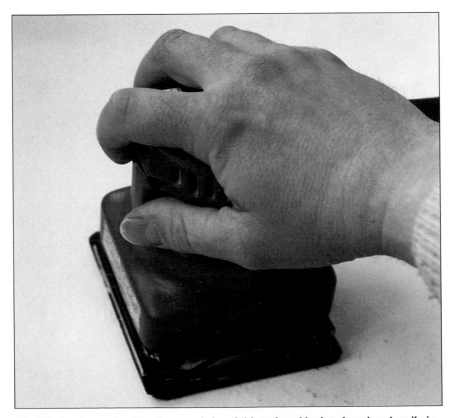

Fig 2.5 A palm sander. The shape and size of this tool enables it to be gripped easily in one hand.

button which, when depressed, keeps the motor running without using the trigger switch. This has the obvious advantage of preventing hand fatigue during periods of extended operation, but it should be used with caution due to the danger of losing your grip on the machine, which would not then automatically turn off.

It is vital that sanders be held correctly and control maintained at all times. Fig 2.6 shows how both hands are used to keep the sanding area in contact with the surface. Take particular care when the machine reaches the ends and edges, to prevent it from dropping over. Fig 2.7 shows how light pressure is transferred from one hand to the other as the sander reaches the ends. The positioning of the hands in Fig 2.6 is the same for orbital sanders, though not of course palm sanders which are operated with one hand only.

There are three other areas of concern when using machinery of this type: electrical safety, noise, and dust.

ELECTRICAL SAFETY

Modern electrical safety standards dictate that machines are double insulated and that the power and

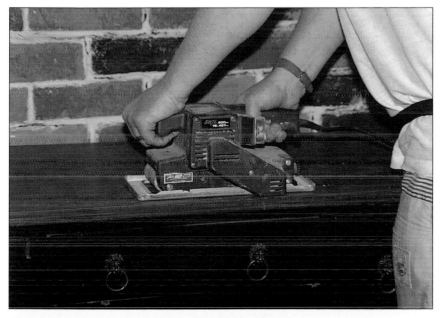

Fig 2.6 The correct way to hold belt and orbital sanders.

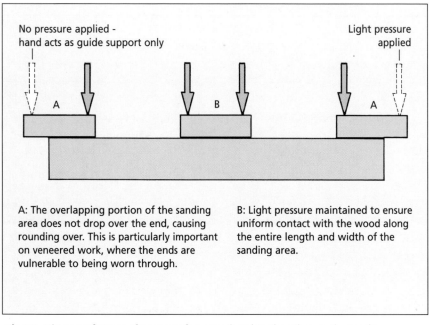

No pressure applied -
hand acts as guide support only

Light pressure
applied

A: The overlapping portion of the sanding
area does not drop over the end, causing
rounding over. This is particularly important
on veneered work, where the ends are
vulnerable to being worn through.

B: Light pressure maintained to ensure
uniform contact with the wood along
the entire length and width of the
sanding area.

Fig 2.7 The transference of pressure from one hand to the other as the sander approaches the ends of the work.

the operator are kept well apart. The cases of hand power tools are now plastic, affording additional protection. However, never use a machine where it is likely to come into contact with water, and employ a circuit breaker to guard against the consequences of snagging the cable with the abrasive.

NOISE

The effect of noise must not be ignored. It is cumulative and generally irreversible. Extended periods of machine noise can damage your hearing, and the use of a noise attenuator is a must. These fit over your ears rather like headphones, and reduce the level of machine noise without deafening you to other sounds. You can hold a perfectly intelligible conversation while still wearing an attenuator.

DUST

The effect of dust is also cumulative in its damaging effect upon the lungs. Always wear a mask and eyeshields in case anything is thrown up by the machine. See Chapter 11 for more on health and safety.

3

SURFACE
PREPARATION

No matter how much care you take in applying a finish, if the surface itself is not adequately prepared to receive it, the end result will be, at the very least, disappointing.

This is because a finish not only protects the wood's surface, but also highlights any blemishes on it. This is especially true of gloss finishes: French polishing, for instance, quickly shows up any deficiencies in craftsmanship – its mirror-like lustre can only be achieved on a perfectly smooth surface, and the slightest blemish will ruin the effect.

A brief explanation of optics will help to illustrate this. A smooth polished surface acts as a mirror, reflecting light to our eyes so that we see a reflection of objects (see Fig 3.1). Fig 3.2 illustrates the effect of a blemish, in this case a small planing tear in the surface fibres of the wood. In effect, the blemish creates many different reflective surfaces, all at different angles to each other, and each reflects light in a different direction. The result is that the blemish scatters light and so produces a break in the otherwise perfect reflection from the rest of the surface. Sometimes these blemishes do not appear to exist until you start applying the finish, at which point they reveal themselves in a manner that makes you believe that the whole thing was a conspiracy to catch you out! In fact, an unpolished surface is not a good reflector of light, so you do not always notice these blemishes. However, they cannot escape your sense of touch, so during the preparation of the surface, slowly run your fingers over the work without applying any pressure, and put your eye-level close to the surface (see Fig 3.3); looking obliquely at a low angle is more revealing than looking directly from above. The combination of sight and touch is formidable.

There is a fairly widespread misconception that a surface defect can somehow be masked with stain and polish, as if to 'paint' it out. While there is a technique used by professional polishers to mask certain blemishes, it is generally untrue that you can 'paper over the cracks' they need to be repaired.

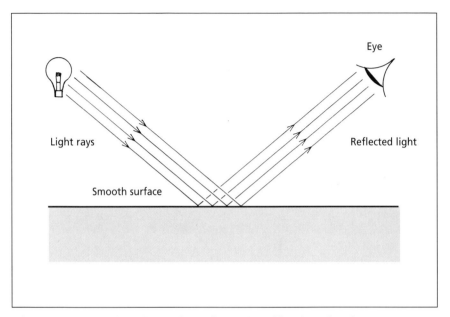

Fig 3.1 A smooth, mirror-like surface reflects light uniformly so that the eye sees perfect reflections.

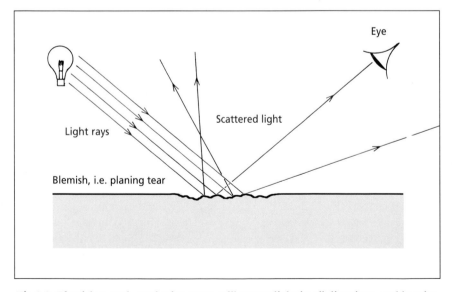

Fig 3.2 Blemishes, such as planing tears, will scatter light in all directions, making the area appear darker and duller because less light reaches the eye.

Fig 3.3 Examining a surface against the light to detect blemishes with a combination of touch and sight.

SMOOTHING TOOLS

It is rare for a piece of wood to be smooth enough to polish direct from a plane iron. There are usually a number of marks caused by the plane, such as tears or undulations (due to the curved nature of jack and fore plane irons), or the occasional ridge caused by a chip in the edge of the iron. Machine-planed timber is even less likely to be suitable for polishing direct from the knives (see Fig 3.4).

Bruises, marking knife lines and pencil marks, not to mention grime from constant handling, all need to be removed. Rather than using abrasive papers, which would take a long time, there are two tools made for the job of cleaning up the work prior to staining and polishing.

Ripples caused by rotating plane knives

Fig 3.4 Exaggerated view of rippled effect sometimes caused by machine planing.

SMOOTHING PLANE

This tool is quite small, being around 9in (229mm) long. It is not designed to remove heavy shavings because, as its name implies, its main function is to enhance a surface by removing light surface blemishes, such as dirt and tool marks.

The iron should be extremely sharp and set very fine, to take shavings so thin as to be almost transparent. The edge of the iron should be perfectly square, with the ends slightly rounded to prevent them from digging in.

On difficult timbers, where the grain is running in more than one direction, take extra care not to plane against the grain. This might mean changing the direction of the planing to minimize the amount of tearing. Fig 3.5 shows typical grain configurations and how to plane them.

CABINET SCRAPER

This simple but extremely effective tool (shown in Fig 3.12) seems to cause problems out of all proportion to its simplicity. Despite its name it is a cutting, not a scraping, tool. It must produce tiny shavings, not dust. It is made of tool steel and is thin enough to be flexible, but hard enough to take a burr on its long edges. Cabinet scrapers come in a variety of shapes and sizes. Fig 3.6 shows the basic shapes: rectangular for flat surfaces; 'goose-necked' for hollows of various radii; and with one end for convex surfaces and the other for shallow hollows. The latter two are used for parts that a smoothing plane cannot reach.

Cabinet scrapers are not very effective on softwoods, as the softness of the fibres makes the surface spring under the pressure of the scraper so that hardly any cutting takes place. On hardwoods however they are extremely effective.

SHARPENING A SCRAPER

Sharpening this tool is a knack which is not difficult to master provided you understand the basic principle behind the technique. In essence, you are producing an edge which is straight, square across its width and burnished smooth of any marks. This edge is then 'turned' to produce a burr, which is what actually cuts the wood.

Even a brand-new scraper needs to be sharpened. Hold it in a vice with a long edge horizontal. With a fine metal file, produce a straight edge which is square across (see Fig 3.7), then draw-file to remove marks made by the teeth (see Fig 3.8). Now burnish the edge on a fine oil or water stone to remove all

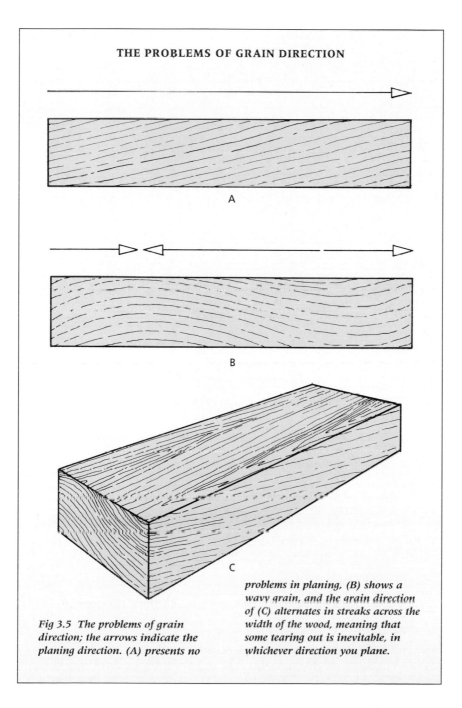

THE PROBLEMS OF GRAIN DIRECTION

A

B

C

Fig 3.5 The problems of grain direction; the arrows indicate the planing direction. (A) presents no problems in planing, (B) shows a wavy grain, and the grain direction of (C) alternates in streaks across the width of the wood, meaning that some tearing out is inevitable, in whichever direction you plane.

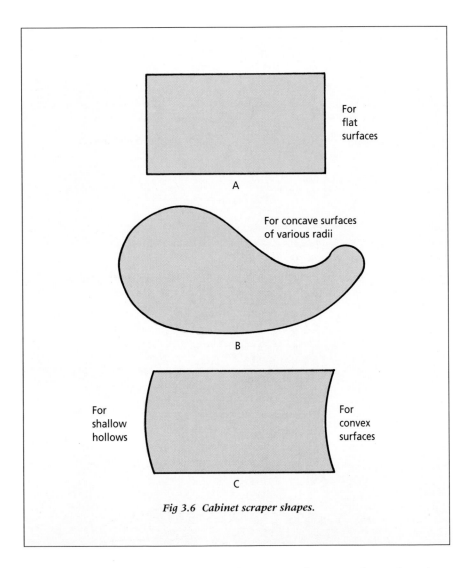

For
flat
surfaces

A

For concave surfaces
of various radii

B

For
shallow
hollows

For
convex
surfaces

C

Fig 3.6 Cabinet scraper shapes.

traces of file marks (see Fig 3.9). There will now be a rough burr on the edge, which is levelled off by rubbing the sides of the scraper on the stone (see Fig 3.10). This procedure is repeated on the other long edge.

A new burr must be made, using a 'burnisher' made of high-speed steel rod ($\frac{1}{4}$–$\frac{3}{8}$in diameter – 6–10mm) mounted in a wooden handle. The rod is held horizontal and drawn hard along each long edge once. It is then drawn along each edge about 5° from the horizontal on both sides of the edge to produce the burr (see Fig 3.11). The new scraper is now ready for use. For future sharpening the four old burrs need to be removed first, by honing the flat faces on the fine stone.

The shaped scrapers cannot be sharpened in this way. Instead, remove the old burrs by honing and burnish the edge for turning using fine Carborundum paper wrapped around a wooden dowel. Then turn the edges in the same manner with the burnisher.

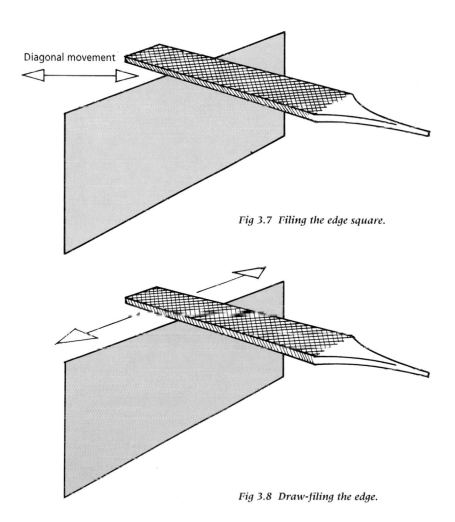

Diagonal movement

Fig 3.7 Filing the edge square.

Fig 3.8 Draw-filing the edge.

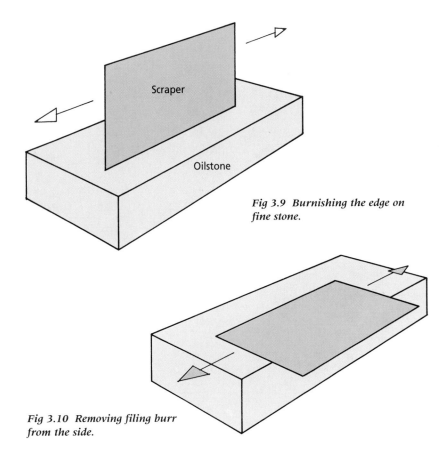

Fig 3.9 *Burnishing the edge on fine stone.*

Fig 3.10 *Removing filing burr from the side.*

USING THE SCRAPER

Hold the scraper as shown in Fig 3.12, with both thumbs flexing the centre and the fingers of both hands curled around the short edges to support it. Push the blade along the surface, tilted just off the vertical so that the burr cuts. A guillotining action is required, with the blade set slightly skew to the direction of cut (always along the grain!). This eases the cutting action, but also means that some of the blade will be on the wood at the end of the stroke so it is supported and the edge of the wood is not damaged by the scraper falling off. If possible, always take long strokes from one end of the wood to the other to prevent hollowing of the surface and reduce the risk of marking. The scraper can get very hot during use; wear sticking plasters on your thumbs to protect them.

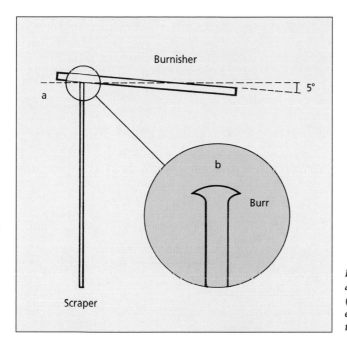

Burnisher

5°

a

b

Burr

Scraper

Fig 3.11 Producing a turned edge, and (detail) an exaggerated view of the edge.

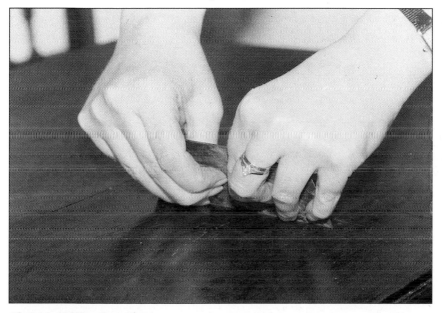

Fig 3.12 Holding the scraper.

If the scraper has been correctly sharpened, very fine shavings will be produced and on very hard woods the surface will take on a sheen as it is smoothed. For very difficult grain configurations, a scraper is an alternative to the smoothing plane, as it does not tear out the fibres. In all other cases it should be used after the plane.

ABRASIVES

On the back of abrasive paper you will see numbers and codes, which refer to the coarseness of the abrasive. The important number is the grit size, as this is the only one which is consistent across the different brands (see Table 2). The higher the number, the finer the particles. For the finisher, the important grit sizes range from 150 for initial preparation through to 320 for ultra-smooth surfaces ready for polishing.

Abrasive papers come in two main weights, A and C (see Fig 3.13). A-weight paper is fairly lightweight, with closely spaced particles and thin backing paper, and is designed for hand sanding. C-weight is heavier, with thick backing paper and the particles further apart, and is used on sanding machines.

There are a number of abrasive products in common use:

TABLE 2

GRIT SIZE	GLASSPAPER CODES	GRADE
320	–	9/0
280	–	8/0
240	–	7/0
220	00	6/0
150	0	4/0
120	1	3/0
100	1½	2/0
80	F2	0
60	M2	½
50	S2	1
30	2½	1½
24	3	2

Table 2 *Comparison of abrasive grading codes appropriate for woodfinishing.*

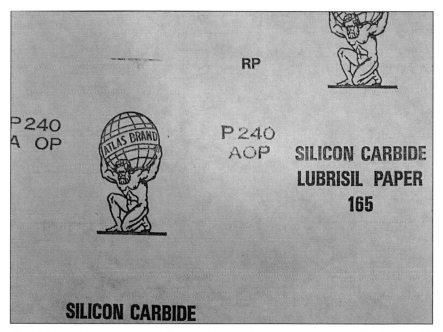

Fig 3.13 The backing paper of all abrasives provides information about the abrasive. In this case, the Lubrisil is A-weight (ideal for hand sanding), and has a fine grit (240).

GLASSPAPER

Particles of ground glass are bonded on to the paper to produce the abrasive surface. This is not a very good abrasive as the particles quickly lose their edge.

GARNET PAPER

A long-lasting paper which uses crushed garnet stone as the abrasive. It is very good value for money, has a good cut on bare and polished wood, and is suitable for initial preparation and 'cutting back' the first coat or two of polish. Cutting back is the term used to describe smoothing a polished surface with abrasive to remove its shine and eliminate any blemishes that may be present. The process also creates a surface that another coat of polish will find easier to bond with.

ALUMINIUM OXIDE

Also known as production paper, this mineral is hard enough to be used on metal. Again, it is very long-lasting and good value for money.

SILICON CARBIDE

This is the hardest of the common abrasive papers and comes in a waterproof version known as wet-or-dry. It is expensive but obtainable in grit sizes down to 1200, ideal for cutting back rubber burns during French polishing (see Chapter 6). Use the 600 grit, wet, for rubbing down between coats of French polish, polyurethane or yacht varnish, to produce a very fine finish.

LUBRISIL

This is an ideal paper for woodturners as it contains its own lubricant that reduces clogging when used at the high speeds associated with lathe work. It is expensive, but very long-lasting if treated well.

NYLON MESH ABRASIVE PADS

A recent innovation, the ultra-fine grade (grit sizes do not apply) is very useful for smoothing between coats of French polish (see Fig 3.14).

PREPARING A SURFACE

The best smoothing method is determined to a large degree by the nature of the surface. There are three broad categories of surface, as follows:

NEW, SOLID WOOD

Use a smoothing plane initially and, for hardwoods, finish off with a cabinet scraper. For coarse-grained

Fig 3.14 This mesh abrasive by Scotch is very long-lasting and is of great advantage when sanding shaped surfaces such as banister rails.

timbers such as oak and ash, which are to be waxed or oiled, the surface is usually suitable to receive polish direct from the scraper blade. For any other finish, such timbers must be sanded.

If a scraper has not been used, begin with a grit size of 150. Take extra care when sanding panelled work where adjoining members have different grain directions (e.g. rails and stiles; see Fig 3.15). Fig 3.15 shows the order of sanding the members of panelled work; any accidental cross-sanding at the joints will be eliminated later on.

Dust off the work regularly, and change to a finer grit each time the paper seems to be gliding over the surface. Move from 150 to 180 and finish with 240 grit. If the wood is particularly fine-grained (e.g. sycamore or satinwood), or you intend to French polish the work, finish off with 320 grit. In all cases, the wood should end up with a definite sheen, indicating it is sufficiently smooth.

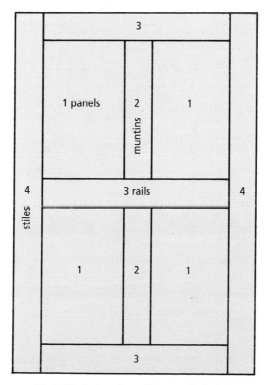

Fig 3.15 Order of sanding panelled work.

Always use a cork rubber (a cork block around which the abrasive paper is wrapped, see Fig 3.16) on large flat surfaces, taking long strokes and working the whole area once before beginning again. This prevents localized hollows. Always take care not to dwell on any particular area but work evenly across the whole surface.

When sanding mouldings use a sanding block of the reverse profile or a nylon mesh abrasive which will mould itself into the profile. Otherwise moulding profiles can be damaged or destroyed by careless use of the paper.

VENEERED WORK

As mentioned before, veneers are thin, making it easy to sand straight through to the substrate beneath. They may also exhibit bubbles or lifting edges at veneer joints, which must be remedied before continuing. There should be no need for coarse abrasives; use 240 grit, quickly followed by 320.

Marquetry, quartered and inlaid work will have grain running in different directions, and as it is not feasible to keep changing the direction of sanding, start with 240 grit to reduce the risk of cross-

Fig 3.16 A cork rubber provides the best means of sanding flat surfaces.

sanding marks showing through the final polish.

If dark and light veneers appear together in a piece dust down regularly to prevent the light veneer turning dark as dust from the dark veneer is forced into it. When you have finished, use a blast of compressed air to clear out the grain if this is available. Sources of air may be a DIY spray gun and compressor kit, or an air brush, which can be bought from art and craft shops. Both are operated by canisters of compressed gas.

Failing this, some vacuum cleaners allow air to be blown, and a blast of air from one of these is just as satisfactory. Do *not* use a damp rag, as this will fix the dust in the grain, not remove it!

STRIPPED SURFACES

Such surfaces have already been through a process of surface preparation before receiving the finish that has just been stripped. They are therefore different to new surfaces in a number of respects.

Stripped surfaces will be smoother, and a fine grit of 240 or 320 should be sufficient, even if water has been used in the stripping process, which can tend to make the wood a little fuzzy. Do not sand any more than necessary.

TREATMENT OF SCRATCHES AND DENTS

The wood may also have acquired scratches and dents during its life and you must decide if they should remain. If they are not disfiguring and will not prevent you from achieving the finish you require, leave them. For those you feel cannot be left because they are too serious, see 'Final preparations'.

FINAL PREPARATIONS

If you intend to use a water-based stain, the surface needs to be moistened with warm water and allowed to dry, to forestall any tendency for the stain to swell the fibres of the wood. By allowing the fibres to swell at this stage, and then sanding with 320 grit paper, little or no swelling is likely after application of the stain, at which stage you would be unable to cut back the raised fibre without making the stain very patchy.

Do not try to fill shallow depressions, as it is always detectable, may look worse than the damage, and will probably fall out anyway. For those blemishes which do need filling, choose the filler according to the intended finish. If waxing, use a coloured wax stick (beaumontage), which you can make yourself (see Chapter 12) or purchase ready made. Melt the wax into the blemish using the tang of a file heated by a spirit burner (see Fig 3.17). If French polishing, melt a shellac stick into the blemish in a similar way. Fill the blemishes proud of the surface and when hardened level off the filler with a sharp chisel. For most other finishes, proprietary 'stoppers' are available. A stopper is a paste made up of a material that has been formulated to fill holes without shrinking as it dries. They are often sold as 'wood filler' and are available in a variety of colours to represent different species of wood. Most will also take stain, but it is wise to check the information on the packaging to be certain of this.

For depressions which you feel will damage the appearance of the piece but which are too shallow to be filled, use the steaming method: place a clean wet cloth over the depression and press a hot clothes iron on to it. The steam generated will be forced into the compressed fibres, causing them to swell, although two or three attempts may be required. When the area is dry, smooth with a fine abrasive paper. Note that this technique cannot be used on veneered work, as the steam will almost certainly damage the glue and cause the veneer to lift.

Finally, you may prefer to carry out filling after staining, when it will be easier to match the colour to the stain. This approach requires great care when levelling the filler, to avoid cutting through the stain.

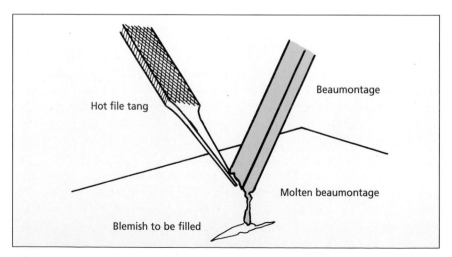

Fig 3.17 Melting beaumontage into a deep blemish.

4

STAINING AND BLEACHING

There are still some suspicions surrounding the use of staining materials in woodworking – in a few cases people still believe you are trying to hide something! In the vast majority of instances, however, staining is a matter of fashion, taste, or plain convention, and of course also has practical values.

CHANGING THE COLOUR

The following are, in my view, legitimate reasons for wanting to change the colour of wood:

UNIFORMITY

As a natural material wood exhibits variations in colour. Wood used from different sources, and even parts of the same tree can vary in colour to a significant degree. If this does not suit your purpose, staining (or bleaching) are legitimate means of achieving uniformity.

DISGUISE

You may wish to make a perfectly good piece of wood resemble a different species. For example, beech is ideal for chair frames and similar pieces which require structural strength; it is hard, close-grained, but incredibly boring to look at. By staining it to resemble mahogany, walnut or oak, the piece can be made interesting to view.

PROTECTION

In Chapter 10, the use of preservative materials is discussed in detail, and the one thing in common with all those pieces designed for exterior use is that they are heavily coloured with special chemicals to protect them against the damage of ultraviolet (UV) light from the sun. Without this, such timbers would quickly disintegrate as the fibres broke down as a result of the chemical effect of UV on organic material.

STAINING MATERIALS

The following staining materials, along with their characteristics and pitfalls, are those most likely to be encountered by the home craftsman and the professional polisher.

OIL STAINS

Whilst expensive, these are still by far the most commonly used product, based on white spirit as the solvent, with a binder to hold the colour in the wood once the solvent has dried. In effect, they are very weak varnishes. This means that only one coat should be applied, for two reasons:

▌ Successive coats produce a surface film which looks like varnish.
▌ You run the risk of dissolving the binder and lifting the colour out of the wood, creating a patchy effect (particularly if you have not allowed sufficient drying time).

However, the advantages of oil stains are:

▌ They are relatively easy to use, producing a generally uniform colour.
▌ They are produced in a range of standard colours, like paint, and each brand has its own colour chart.
▌ They have good penetration and coverage.
▌ They can be applied by brush or pad (see 'Applying stains' on page 39).

Always bear in mind that samples of standard oil stain colours are usually on plywood or pine, which are initially very light in colour. As with all stains, remember that the colour of the stain will be modified by the colour of the wood. For example, you may find that a 'walnut' stain looks better on mahogany than a 'mahogany' stain. Test the colour first on an appropriate piece of scrap wood, or on an inconspicuous area of the piece in question (see Fig 4.1).

The colour range available can of course be extended by mixing different colours, but always keep to the same brand, as they do not all have the same composition.

During use it helps to decant the stain into a wide-necked container, but do not use plastic as the solvent may dissolve it, and will certainly dissolve such items as margarine tubs or disposable plastic cups!

A disadvantage of oil stains is that application of polyurethane varnish or wax polish may cause bleeding of the colour by dissolving the binder. It is therefore important to give the work a brush coat of transparent French polish before using wax or varnish, to create an isolating film.

The most well-known brands of these stains are known as 'wood dyes' and include such household names on the DIY market as Colron and Blackfriars. They are universally available in all good DIY shops.

Fig 4.1 Testing a stain on scrap wood. The test piece is offered up to the main work to assess the colour match.

ACRYLIC DYES

These are the latest generation of dyes and are water-based, using an acrylic polymer as the binder. They are ideal for use underneath the equally new generation of acrylic varnishes. Their advantages are:

- They are fast-drying.
- They have a large coverage.
- They produce softer colours, a characteristic of all water-based dyes.
- They are compatible with all finishes.
- They can be applied by brush or pad (see 'Applying stains' on page 39).

As these dyes are water-based, there is a risk of grain raising as described on page 31 in Chapter 3. My own experience indicates that this is not an enormous problem as such dyes contain an anti-grain-raising ingredient.

ANILINE DYES

These are available in both powder and liquid concentrate form as single colours (e.g. red, blue, green, yellow), or ready-mixed to specific wood colours. There are two types: one uses methylated spirit as the solvent, the other uses water. Spirit dyes are useful for tinting French polish for the purpose of colouring (see Chapter 8). They are also good for hiding scratches on furniture when applied with a small artist's brush. They are not ideal for staining large surfaces, because their drying time is so short that it is difficult to avoid creating tidemarks.

The dyes can be mixed to produce custom-made colours, but the two types of dye cannot be mixed together; i.e. you must only mix spirit with spirit and water with water. If you are using powdered dyes, you will need to dissolve the powder in the appropriate solvent beforehand. Be warned: these dyes are very strong, and a small amount goes a long way. A teaspoon in a pint (560ml) of water or methylated spirit is about right for most purposes.

As you can see, a relatively small quantity of powder will make an enormous amount of stain, and it is probably more cost-effective to buy liquid concentrate. This is also a more convenient medium, as it can be quickly and easily thinned with its respective solvent as and when required. The powdered form, on the other hand, takes several hours, with regular shaking, to dissolve thoroughly and be ready for use.

The water-based dyes are very useful, especially for restoration work, because of the ability to create your own colours for colour matching. Equally, because of their intensity and the range of colours available, it is possible to be adventurous in the colouring of wood, creating a whole range of special effects.

Before choosing aniline dyes, do bear in mind the fact that they are not particularly colour fast, and may fade fairly quickly if exposed to strong sunlight. This is especially true of spirit dyes.

VANDYKE CRYSTALS

Sometimes referred to as walnut crystals, these are produced by pressing out the juice from unripe walnut shells, and are water-soluble. They produce a basic chestnut brown traditionally used on walnut and oak, but, according to concentration, the depth of colour can be varied from honey to black.

The crystals are difficult to dissolve, and this process can be eased by using the following method:

1 Mix the crystals to a paste with hot water.
2 Gradually add more hot water to dissolve the paste.
3 Add a dash of ammonia to aid penetration.
4 Test the colour and adjust the concentration as required.
5 Store in a wide-necked jar.

As the water cools, some of the crystals will come out of solution and form sediment at the bottom of the jar, which can be retrieved later and redissolved in more hot water.

Very concentrated solutions can have a tendency to be sticky, leading

SALES DRAFT

HALF PRICE BOOKS #052
1375 W LANE AVE
COLUMBUS, OH 432210000
TERMINAL 5691845

324022152999
06/29/2003   17:10:46
MC XXXXXXXXXXXX2135
AUTH. TRANS. ID.   MCC00HQJJ
INVOICE   08103 H02
AUTH. CODE   596088

SALE TOTAL $31.12

CUSTOMER COPY

to streakiness, but the stain can be wiped off the wood with a wet rag, allowing colour adjustment to be carried out. This will also enable you to simulate the effects of age by making light and dark areas, to resemble wear. I find this material invaluable as a general purpose brown stain.

CHEMICAL STAINS

The above stains may be legitimately referred to as dyes (and are often sold as such), while true staining (i.e. actually changing the colour of the wood by chemical change) is achieved with chemicals which, when applied to the surface, react with substances in the wood itself. Not all woods will respond, and even those that do may not stain evenly, because the action depends very much on the concentration of chemicals (notably tannic acid) present in the wood. Because they depend on a chemical reaction for their staining effect, the colour of the stains bears no relation to the final colour achieved.

The most commonly used chemical stains and their actions are:

BICHROMATE OF POTASH
This is orange in colour and a solution of 2oz (56.7g) in a pint of warm water will turn mahogany a

red/brown, and oak a warm, mellow brown.

IRON SALTS
In weak solutions these give a silvery tone to oak, and may also be used to kill the redness of mahogany if you want to stain it to resemble walnut. The salts produce a greyish tone on sycamore to create 'harewood' (especially useful in marquetry and the like). If used in too strong a mixture, iron salts will turn oak inky black. If you steep iron nails in white vinegar overnight and decant off the liquid, you will have a stock solution of iron acetate which can be used to create harewood, or applied to oak to turn it almost black. The latter is useful when attempting to recreate ancient oak, which proprietary wood dyes just cannot do. However, be warned – its effect on colour can be unpredictable, so test it on an offcut of the oak first.

AMMONIA
The strongest solution available is called 'point eight eighty' (0.880), and is 35% ammonia. (Household ammonia is between 5% and 15% concentration.) On its own the 35% solution creates only a slight darkening of oak, but if this wood is exposed to ammonia fumes the effect is dramatic. The oak progressively darkens and

eventually turns grey-black. The process can be stopped at any point by ending the exposure. The resulting oak looks very old and ammonia can therefore be used when restoring old oak timbers and artefacts.

This method is really only suitable for small articles, which should be placed under an upturned fish tank, which allows you to observe the process without exposing yourself to the fumes. Pour a little ammonia into a non-metallic container such as a saucer or margarine tub, and place this under the tank. The process is slow, and you will need to keep an eye on the work. Gradually, the oak will begin to darken, first going a mellow brown, then grey and eventually black. When you are satisfied with the colour, remove the item from the tank and allow it to air for a while before finishing.

When using ammonia it is essential to protect yourself adequately from its toxicity and the effect of the fumes; see 'Health and safety when staining and bleaching' and Chapter 11.

OTHER STRONG ALKALIS

Caustic soda, washing soda and other strong alkalis will darken oak, mahogany and other hardwoods, which is one reason for not using caustic stripping on these timbers. 1oz to a pint of clean water (28.35g to 0.56l) is a good solution for these chemicals, which can be strengthened or diluted as necessary. Add the caustic granules gradually to cold water in a bucket, stirring all the time. A great deal of heat is generated, so wait for the solution to cool down before using. Do bear in mind that all strong alkalis can dissolve brushes!

HEALTH AND SAFETY WHEN STAINING AND BLEACHING

All stains should be considered as toxic materials and treated as such. Store them in properly labelled containers and keep them locked away from children and animals.

They should also be considered as irritants (many stains can lead to contact dermatitis), so it is essential to wear protective clothing and rubber gloves. Goggles should also be worn when mixing and using ammonia and caustic soda, and in the case of ammonia you must also wear a respirator fitted with a gas cartridge. Ammonia fumes are overpowering and can cause damage to your lungs, especially if you are asthmatic or bronchitic. See Chapter 11 for more detail on protective clothing and equipment.

APPLYING STAINS

There are two methods: brush and pad.

BRUSH

Decant the stain into a wide-necked container. Only use paintbrushes reserved for the sole purpose of staining. Charge your brush and squeeze out surplus from the bristle tips by pressing against the side of the container. On large flat areas such as table tops, apply the stain in straight strokes along the grain, working from the edge furthest away from you and gradually moving towards you. Overlap the strokes slightly, as shown in Fig 4.2, so that only one 'live' edge is kept open, thus preventing tide-marks. Recharge the brush as required. When the whole surface has been covered, take a clean, lint-free rag, dip it into the stain and thoroughly wring it out. Form the rag into a pad and wipe over the work, in straight strokes along the grain, to even out the colour. Allow to dry.

Break down the work into manageable sections. Do not try to stain a large piece all at once, as the stain will dry before you can even it out. On a table, for example, treat the top as one section, the legs as another, and so on. A second coat may be applied after the first has dried.

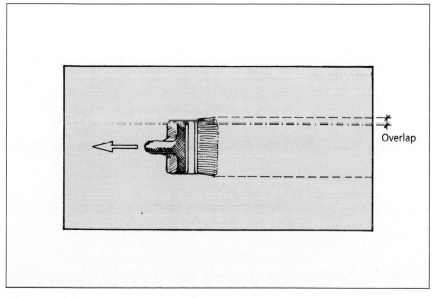

Fig 4.2 Staining by brush. Note the slight overlap between strokes.

Intricate mouldings and carvings may require a stabbing action with the brush to ensure no spots are missed. Missed spots can however be touched up, using a pencil brush. Such brushes are also used to apply French polish to inaccessible areas, and one is illustrated in Fig 6.19 in Chapter 6, which discusses French polishing in detail.

PAD

This method can really only be used satisfactorily on flat surfaces. Fold some upholstery wadding into a ball, wrap it in a clean, lint-free cotton rag and flatten the face to form a pad, shown in Fig 4.3.

Staining pads are able to hold more stain than an ordinary piece of cloth, and consequently act as a reservoir when covering large, flat surfaces (see Fig 4.4).

Dip the pad into the stain and allow it to draw up into the wadding. Squeeze the pad against the side to remove surplus and work the stain over the surface in a circular motion, shown in Fig 4.5. Apply little or no pressure at first, as the stain will flow freely on to the work, but gradually increase pressure as the pad dries out. Recharge the pad as necessary, and finish off by working along the grain as shown in Fig 4.6, to eliminate the circular paths and even out the colour.

Fig 4.3 Staining pad.

Fig 4.4 A staining pad holds more stain than a piece of ordinary cloth, and acts as a reservoir when covering a large, flat surface.

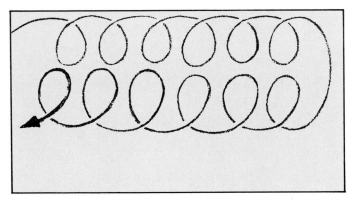

Fig 4.5 The circular path adopted when applying stain by pad.

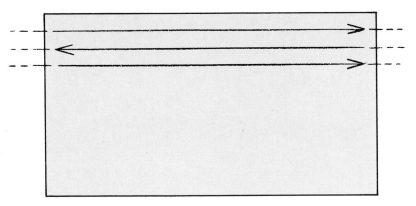

Fig 4.6 The straight strokes of the staining pad.

STAINING PANELLED WORK

Fig 4.7 shows the correct order in which panelled work should be stained. Use a brush for such work, and be wary of runs.

BLEACHING WOOD

Sometimes you will need to eliminate stain marks and the like before dyeing the wood, or you may wish to remove as much colour from the wood as possible. Both cases involve bleaching. In the first case a stain needs to be removed without creating a light patch, for which oxalic acid should be used. The second requires a chemical action to penetrate the wood; a two-part wood bleach is the most suitable for this.

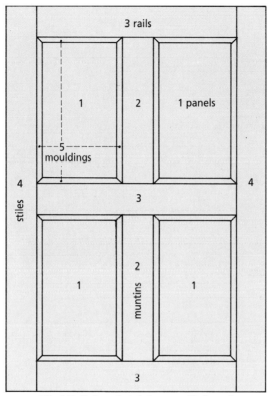

Fig 4.7 Order of staining panelled work.

OXALIC ACID

This is a toxic organic acid
obtainable through pharmacists.
Always wear gloves during use and
store the acid in a safe place in well-
labelled containers.

The process of bleaching out a
stain using oxalic acid is as follows:

1 Make sure the surface has been
   stripped of any kind of finish.
2 Make up a solution of
   approximately 2oz in a pint of
   warm water (56.7g in 0.56l).
3 Sponge over the whole surface,
   and allow to dry thoroughly.
4 Once dry, you may find a whitish
   deposit on the surface. This is
   crystals of oxalic acid, which can
   be brushed off – wear a mask
   during this process to avoid
   inhaling the crystals.
5 Neutralize any residual acid in
   the wood with a solution of 1oz
   borax in a pint of warm water
   (28.35g in 0.56l). Sponge this
   solution on and allow to dry.

If the surface is a little fuzzy after neutralizing, due to raised grain, give it a very light sand before staining and finishing. Fig 4.8 shows before and after photographs of the effect of oxalic acid on an ink stain.

TWO-PART WOOD BLEACH

Chemically speaking, oxygen is an extremely active substance. When produced during a chemical reaction, it is so chemically active

Fig 4.8 Before and after bleaching an ink stain. Sometimes more than one application is needed, and in this case two applications were required.

that it readily attacks organic materials as well as metals. The chemicals in wood that produce its colour are highly sensitive, and by producing oxygen gas within the wood via a chemical reaction, they are attacked and changed to a near-colourless state. This is known as an oxidation reaction.

Two-part bleaches comprise two chemicals: a strong alkali (usually 2% caustic soda) and a strong solution of hydrogen peroxide (typically 100 vol.). They can be bought individually through a pharmacy, but it is better to buy a proprietary wood bleach which will have been specially formulated.

Always read individual brands' instructions, as they may vary, but the following outlines the process in principle:

1 Brush the first solution over the wood, taking care not to flood it, and leave for about five minutes. As this is a strong alkali some hardwoods may darken considerably; don't panic, this is quite normal!
2 Brush the second solution over the wood and leave to dry. The hydrogen peroxide may cause frothing after a few minutes which is also quite normal. This is the oxygen being released from the peroxide, which might also create sizzling sounds.
3 Leave for two or three days to thoroughly dry out. The wood will now be fuzzy due to raised grain and some watermarks may be apparent. Gently wash down with a weak solution of white vinegar (which will neutralize the alkali) and leave to dry for another day or so.
4 Gently sand smooth with 320 grit abrasive, and not too deep, as bleaching does not penetrate very far.
5 If the work is not light enough, repeat the process.

Always remember that both these chemicals are dangerous and can cause painful skin burns. Always wear protective clothing, rubber gloves and eye protectors.

Use only synthetic bristle brushes, as the chemicals will dissolve the real thing, and use a separate brush for each solution to avoid contamination. Decant each solution into separate, labelled plastic, glass or ceramic containers, and always discard unused solutions, as these may be contaminated. *Do not pour them back into their original containers; chemical reactions may cause them to explode.*

Never use metal containers; both chemicals will react with the metal, and peroxide in particular will undergo premature chemical breakdown.

PIGMENTS

Pigments are coloured powders that do not dissolve in a liquid. In this respect they are fundamentally different to stains. When stirred into a liquid, the powders remain suspended for a while before settling on the bottom of the container (shown in Fig 4.9).

The role of pigments in finishing is limited, but they can achieve effects unobtainable with stains. For example, if raw umber (which is a dirty, greeny grey) is mixed with wax polish and used on pine, it helps to create an antique effect by collecting in crevices and giving the surface a powdery look associated with age.

Because pigments lie on the surface of the wood they give a granular effect which is well worth experimenting with. However, restrict your colours to the so-called 'earth pigments', used in the process of French polishing and described in Chapter 6 under 'Grainfilling and oiling'.

Fig 4.9 (left) A stain dissolves in the liquid, which is semi-transparent; (right) A pigment will not dissolve, and clouds the liquid. Eventually, the pigment settles out to the bottom of the container. It is important to agitate any pigment-based mixture, to keep it uniformly mixed.

5

WAX AND OIL POLISHING

Apart from paint, wax and oil are probably the oldest forms of wood finishes, which gives them the assumed credentials to claim their place as being the most 'natural' and aesthetically pleasing. However, the same charge can be levelled against them as was made against the indiscriminate use of French polish towards the end of the nineteenth century and the beginning of the twentieth: wax and oil polishes are just as prone to indiscriminate and inappropriate application. 'Rustic' timbers such as oak look good under the low lustre of oil and wax, which leave the tactile surface texture which is so much admired, but many highly figured and richly coloured woods need to have their features brought out by the optical properties of 'hard' finishes such as French polish.

Amongst the most common errors is the attempt to dress varnished, French polished or lacquered furniture with beeswax or furniture oil. The result is a greasy build-up which eventually dulls and masks the surface as it attracts dust and other pollutants from the air.

Remember that beeswax polish and furniture oils such as Danish oil, tung oil and linseed oil are wood finishes in their own right and are not designed to be used with, or on, anything else.

Table 3 compares and contrasts the advantages and disadvantages of wax and oil polishes.

TABLE 3		
QUALITIES	WAX	OIL
Easy to apply	Yes	Yes
Durability	Low	High
Heat and water resistance	Low	High
Renewability and revival	Yes	Yes

The conclusions to be drawn from this information are:

- These polishes are easy to apply so that a high level of practical skills is not required.
- Wax polish is vulnerable and therefore not suitable for projects

which will be subject to a great deal of exposure to heat or moisture.

▌ Oil is highly resistant to moisture and heat and is therefore suitable for use in finishing such pieces as dining and coffee tables.

▌ Both forms of polish are easily renewed or revived by the application of another coat as they wear.

SURFACE PREPARATION

Adopt the procedures described in Chapter 3. If a scraper has been used on oak, polishing can take place without the need for sanding. Hardwoods can be given an initial sheen by means of a process known as 'burnishing'.

A burnisher is made from a piece of hardwood (usually beech), which is very hard, and close-grained. The shape and size of this tool is shown in Fig 5.1. Fig 5.2 shows the burnisher in use. By rubbing the rounded edge along the grain with as much pressure as you and the furniture can stand, the surface fibres are compressed and packed tightly, creating a sheen. Use burnishing to quickly build up a shine on oak or other home-grown hardwoods such as ash or walnut.

Softwoods, such as pine, do not burnish well, and the pressure required can cause indentations.

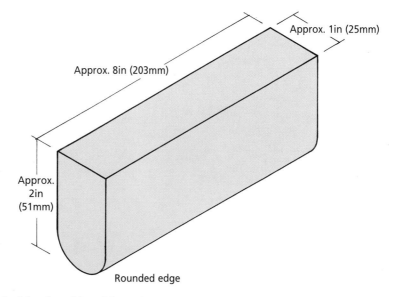

Approx. 1in (25mm)

Approx. 8in (203mm)

Approx. 2in (51mm)

Rounded edge

Fig 5.1 A hardwood burnisher.

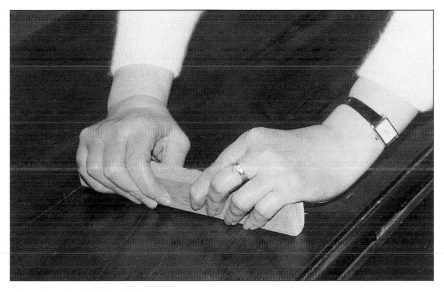

Fig 5.2 Using the burnisher.

WAX POLISHING

Recipes for wax polishes are given in Chapter 12. In essence, they consist of a wax dissolved in a solvent such as turpentine or white spirit. Some formulations rely on a more volatile liquid, akin to petrol, but these products give off dangerous fumes, making use of a respirator essential. They have the advantage of high-speed evaporation making for quick drying.

Wax polishes cannot do their job properly until all the solvent has evaporated and only the wax remains. At this stage, friction is used to soften the wax and distribute it in a smooth, thin and lustrous coat, filling all the pores of the wood and creating an even surface.

There are a number of different waxes available for use singly, or more commonly, in combination:

BEESWAX

This is the best known of the polishing waxes, but while its smell is irresistible, it does have its drawbacks. It is expensive (due to its natural origins), and it tends to become tacky in warm environments, fingermarking easily and attracting dust.

Beeswax can be bought in blocks, and is white (purified wax) or yellow (natural) in colour (see Fig 5.3).

Fig 5.3 Beeswax (left), and Carnauba wax (right). Carnauba wax has the appearance of brittle toffee, and comes in either unpurified (dark) or purified (light) forms.

CARNAUBA WAX

The shiny outer skin of a Brazilian palm is the source of this wax, which is also shown in Fig 5.3. It is very hard and brittle, and as such is rarely used on its own. Traditional beeswax polish can be improved by adding 10% carnauba wax. This stiffens the resulting polish making it more durable and harder when dry, and as carnauba wax is harder it produces a deeper sheen than beeswax would on its own.

PARAFFIN WAX

Commonly known as candle wax, this cannot be regarded as a polish in itself, but may be used in cheaper polishes to make them less expensive.

JAPAN WAX

This is a very expensive blend of vegetable waxes with exceptional properties. It is to be found in the best traditionally blended wax polishes.

SYNTHETIC WAX

The best known is silicone wax. Synthetic waxes form the basis of many modern formulations of wax polishes. The silicones in particular have the property of imparting a very high sheen in return for relatively little effort. The problem is that they create a high build-up and may even trap dust between the layers during each application. Eventually, instead of improving the shine, this results in the surface becoming dull and patchy.

WAX PASTES AND CREAMS

PASTES

The stiffer wax pastes are produced by simply dissolving the wax in a suitable solvent such as turpentine or white spirit. The wax content is proportionally very high, and the pastes need to be applied quite sparingly to prevent excessive build-up, making the finish difficult to buff.

The consistency of the paste can be varied by altering the relative amounts of solvent and wax: the higher the wax content the stiffer the paste. For the first few applications on to bare wood the paste ought to be fairly soft – the consistency of butter on a warm day. This enables it to be spread more easily and to be forced into the pores of the wood, sealing it effectively. Two or three coats will probably be enough to build up the initial body of wax. Subsequent applications can be made with a stiff paste which tends to buff up to a sheen more easily.

CREAMS

These are formed by emulsifying the wax and solvent mixture in water, resulting in a proportionally much lower wax content than the pastes. They are not designed to be used as a finish in their own right but as a dressing over a hard finish such as French polish to improve lustre and provide a measure of additional protection. Because they contain water and an emulsifying agent, wax creams also have a cleaning action on the surface.

The consistency of a cream varies in stiffness from very liquid to being like whipped cream, and can be made at home, though there are many excellent proprietary brands. If you'd like to try your hand at making your own, see the recipe for beeswax furniture cream in Chapter 12 (page 144).

APPLYING WAX POLISH

Be sparing; the more you use, the more difficult it becomes to obtain good results. Adopt the rule of thumb: two thin applications are always better than one heavy coat.

You will find it useful to seal the surface of softwoods and more open-grained hardwoods such as oak or ash with a coat of transparent French polish. Apply sparingly with a brush and allow to dry for a couple of hours. Sealing reduces the number of wax applications by at least one coat, possibly two, by building up the sheen more quickly. It also helps to reduce long-term dirt penetration.

Wax polish is applied with a cloth which should have an open weave, as the wax is less likely to clog it up. Probably the best cloth to use is stockinette (a soft, double-layered material), which is sold as a roll and can be bought from good DIY shops. It may also be sold under the names 'mutton cloth' or 'polishing cloth', depending on the brand.

Apply the wax using a circular motion, forcing it into the pores of the wood. Finish off with straight strokes along the grain and leave to dry for at least an hour, longer if possible. When dry, buff the surface vigorously along the grain with a new piece of stockinette to bring out the shine. You may find it easier to buff large flat surfaces using a piece of terry towelling wrapped around a brick (see Fig 5.4).

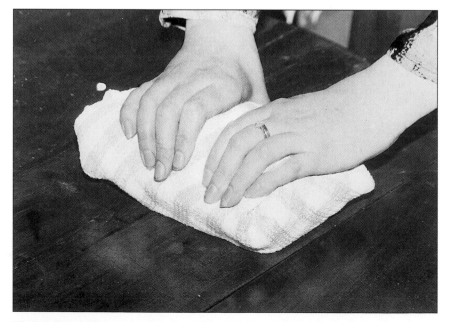

Fig 5.4 Burnishing a waxed surface with an old towel wrapped around a brick.

Carvings need to have the polish applied using a shoebrush, allowed to dry and then be buffed with a clean brush. Try to avoid accumulations of wax in the corners and quirks, as these look unsightly and attract dust. Finally, buff the carving with a clean cloth.

HOW MANY COATS?

Waxing produces a better finish with time, as does oiling. Initially two or three applications will produce an acceptable finish, but as the years go by and more applications are made the wood surface takes on a warm, mellow glow.

OIL POLISHING

Our forebears most commonly used linseed oil as a furniture oil, but they also used other vegetable oils such as poppy, walnut, olive and hazelnut. These remain the traditional oils, linseed oil chief among them, but there are now proprietary products available offering a number of distinct advantages in that they are specially formulated to be easy to apply, become absorbed into the wood faster, and dry more quickly due to the presence of a drier which speeds up the reaction of the oil with oxygen in the air (oxidation).

Proprietary oil blends include teak oil, Danish oil and tung oil.

The main advantage of oiling is that a fully oiled surface is resistant to moisture and heat. A traditional recipe for a polish based on linseed oil is given in Chapter 12 (page 144). Note that *raw* linseed oil is specified, not boiled, which, though it dries faster, is more viscous and therefore slower to be absorbed by the wood. The recipe also includes turpentine or white spirit as a solvent, which dilutes the oil enabling it to be more easily absorbed. Proprietary oils will also contain a solvent.

APPLYING THE OIL

The first coat is best applied with a clean paintbrush. Don't flood the work, but be generous without creating puddles. Leave for 24 hours and then rub vigorously with a lint-free cloth to remove surplus oil from the surface. Apply the second coat sparingly with a cloth and leave for another 24 hours before rubbing over again. At this stage you may begin to see something of a sheen, but the more absorbent the wood the more applications will be required before any real impression is made.

The process can be made more effective by first warming the oil using a double boiler arrangement, shown in Fig 5.5. The heat makes the oil more fluid and aids its absorption by the wood. A similar double boiler can be used for melting wax (see Chapter 12, page 143).

HOW MANY COATS?

It is often said that the job of oil polishing is never finished. There is always room for another coat. As a rule of thumb, for new and stripped surfaces, I follow the regime of one coat a day for a week, followed by one coat a week for a month, followed by one coat a month for a year. By the end of this period the surface will have gained an unmistakable sheen and silky smoothness. After this, oil may be applied as necessary. The test is whether water runs off without penetration!

As time goes by heat or moisture can cause dulling, but this can be remedied with – yes – another coat or two of oil.

Fig 5.5 The double boiler arrangement, here used for oil polishing. Boiling water has been poured into the pan and the metal bowl containing the oil floats on the water. Oil can be warmed very quickly using this method.

6
FRENCH POLISHING

French polishing was introduced into the UK during the first quarter of the nineteenth century, and the practitioners of the craft immediately kept the process a closely guarded secret. The mechanics of the process are actually quite straightforward, but its application is notoriously difficult. At best, any written description can only convey the mechanics, although the odd tip here and there concerning working problems and the like will, I hope, be useful. It is only through practice that the skill can be acquired. Expect disappointing results at first, because there are so many variables that contribute towards a perfect finish, making your early efforts very frustrating. The effort is worth it once you have mastered the skill, though there will of course always be something more to learn.

An important skill in French polishing is restraint in use. There is always a temptation to use it everywhere and create the mirror gloss associated with pianos. A good French polisher is subtle, with the polish itself and with the use of colour.

French polish has its disadvantages: it will not resist heat, water or alcohol, and even exposure to a damp, cold atmosphere over a long period (for example when furniture is in storage) can result in 'blooming'(see page 82).

The benefits of course are obvious: French polish has a smooth and quite unique lustre, and optical effects on colour and figure make it the most attractive of the hard finishes.

WHAT IS FRENCH POLISH?

French polish is a solution of shellac in alcohol. Shellac is a natural product exuded by the insect *laccifer lacca* which is common on the Indian subcontinent.

There are a number of grades of shellac available, according to the degree of processing it has undergone before being made into polish.

There is no real virtue in making your own as proprietary brands are of consistent quality, but should you wish to try, a recipe appears in Chapter 12 (see page 144).

TYPES OF POLISH

GARNET

The darkest of the polishes, made from shellac flakes the colour of garnet stone. When dissolved in alcohol they form a greenish-red/brown polish which is ideal for use over dark or darkly stained woods.

BUTTON

The shellac flakes are a muddy brown colour, and the polish is useful when applied over old walnut which has faded to a honey-brown. However, it tends to give a rather unattractive colour cast on brown or reddish timbers.

WHITE

White is produced by bleaching dark shellac. It creates a creamy-white polish and is useful as a general sealer and as a base for tinted polish. Used as a straight finish, if a deep body of polish is built up it will create a slightly grey colour cast, owing to the natural wax present in shellac. Because of this it should be reserved for light-coloured woods, as a sealer over marquetry, or where the natural colours need to be preserved as much as possible.

TRANSPARENT WHITE (OR PALE)

If the wax is removed from white shellac the resulting polish is a pale amber colour. This tends to be more expensive, because its manufacture is more involved, but it is ideal for use where the colour of the wood is very light or where the colours of inlays and marquetry must be preserved.

OTHER TYPES OF FRENCH POLISH

As well as those described above there are polishes described as 'outside' or 'exterior'. These are harder and more resistant to water, and can be used on doors subjected to a *modest* amount of moisture. They are also useful for table tops if a traditional finish is required. Again, dark and light varieties are available, along with their own thinners if needed. Do not confuse such 'table-top' French polishes with bar top lacquers, which are a totally different product.

FADS AND RUBBERS

What distinguishes French polishing from varnishing is the method of application. The French polisher has two very simple but important tools for building up the sheen: fads and rubbers. Both are deceptively simple, but must be made absolutely correctly.

A fad is a pad of upholstery skin wadding, while a rubber is a similar pad over which is stretched a piece of clean, white, fine-grained cotton.

MAKING A FAD

Read the following description in conjunction with Fig 6.1. A piece of skin wadding approximately 10in (254mm) square is cut and laid on a clean surface, such as white paper. It is folded in half, then folded into thirds, and then the corners folded in to form a point. This point, illustrated in Fig 6.1(e), allows the fad to reach into corners. Upholstery wadding is rather springy, and it may be difficult to manipulate the material. If you first soak the material in French polish and squeeze out as much as possible, the wadding will behave itself and form the required pear shape without too much difficulty.

Once made, the fad can be left to dry out and harden. Before use it is softened in French polish, to 'set' any loose fibres and reduce the risk of them finding their way on to the surface during polishing. In use, the fad is held in the same way as a rubber, shown in Fig 6.3(b).

MAKING A RUBBER

This is the tool most people normally associate with French polishing. It consists of a fad made up as described above, which is then wrapped in fine-grained white cotton – old cotton shirts or sheets are ideal. Fig 6.2 shows how the rag, as it is called, is wrapped around the fad. Note that the point of the fad is maintained to allow the rubber to get into corners.

The method of holding the rubber is extremely important. The bottom needs to be in constant contact with the work, and an even flow of polish through the rag maintained. If held too high up, as in Fig 6.3(a) the rubber will wobble, and you will have too little control, resulting in drag marks (also known as rubber burns) and loss of shape. The rubber should be held as shown in Fig 6.3(b): the face is pressed against the work, giving you greater control, and you will be able to feel what is happening, such as the early signs of drag, or the tell-tale scraping sensation of grit under the rubber.

Rubbers and fads have to be kept on the move at all times to prevent them from sticking. If for any reason you have to stop in mid-stroke, lift the rubber or fad off the surface *without stopping*. Bad burns cannot be removed by trying to cover them up – it only makes them worse. Stop, allow the work to dry for half an hour, then gently rub down before continuing.

Fads and rubbers can be used over and over again if they are

MAKING A FAD

Fig 6.1(a) Folding skin wadding to form a fad. Note the fine-textured, fibrous covering (the skin), which sandwiches the cotton wool.

Fig 6.1(b) Cut a piece roughly 10in (254mm) square.

Fig 6.1(c) Fold in half.

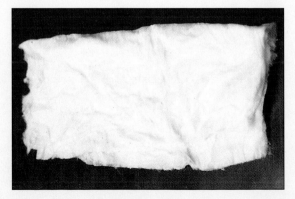

Fig 6.1(d) Divide and fold over into thirds, creating the basic pad.

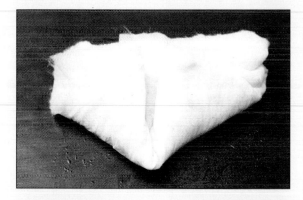

Fig 6.1(e) Form the point along the bullnosed edge by folding in the corners.

Fig 6.1(f) Form the fad into a pear shape by gripping with your hand.

MAKING A RUBBER

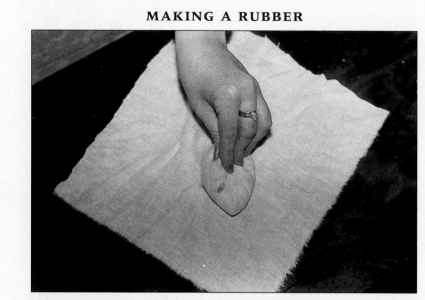

Fig 6.2(a) Align the point of the fad with one of the corners of the rag.

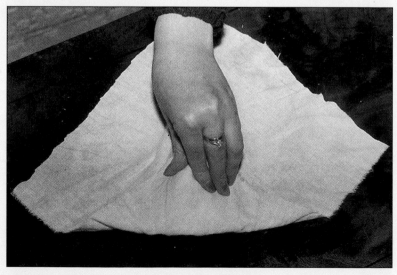

Fig 6.2(a) Bring the corner over the point of the fad.

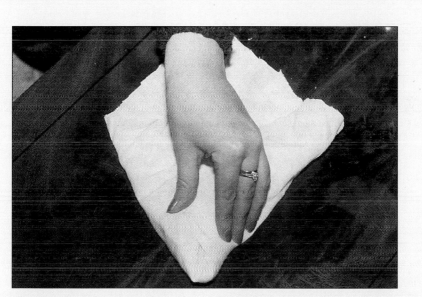

Fig 6.2(c) Wrap the 'wings' of the rag round the point, to define and maintain it.

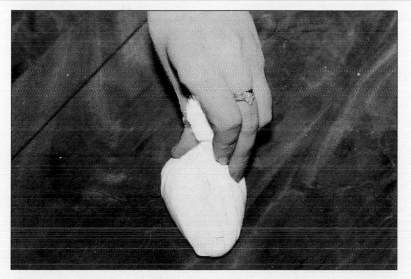

Fig 6.2(d) Twist the 'ends' of the rag around.

HOLDING THE RUBBER

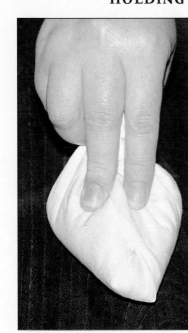

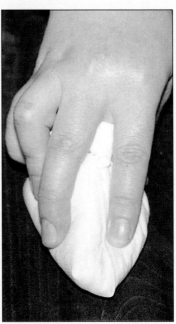

Fig 6.3(a) Holding the rubber too high.

Fig 6.3(b) The correct position, which allows the fingers to support the rubber and maintains good contact with the work.

stored in airtight plastic or glass containers between periods of use, especially between coats, even though the wait might only be a matter of minutes.

THE WORKING ENVIRONMENT

French polish is very sensitive to the environment during its application and for a period of hours afterwards whilst it is hardening. Keep the environmental temperature at around 20°C (68°F) for the whole polishing period (including the time between polishing stages), plus an extra 24 hours to be safe. If the air is allowed to cool, the polish may bloom as moisture condenses on the surface and becomes trapped in it. The air needs to be free of excessive amounts of dust (no dusty jobs while polishing). It is a good idea to have a separate room for polishing work, well away from major sources of dust. After cutting back with abrasives – a frequent event in French polishing – make sure that all dust is removed from the surface, using a 'tack rag' (see below). This is imperative in order to maintain a dust-free environment.

MAKING AND
USING A TACK RAG

Tack rags can be bought ready made, since they are a standard piece of a professional decorator's equipment, from DIY stores and decorator's merchants. However, if you find difficulty in buying one, or would like to make your own in any case, the method is as follows.

You will need a piece of stockinette (see page 52) about 12in (305mm) long. Soak it in water and then wring it out tightly so that it is damp to the touch, rather than wet. Sprinkle white spirit liberally over the cloth and work it through the whole of the material. Finally, sprinkle raw linseed oil over the cloth, and work this through. The cloth will now feel quite wet and should be opened up and allowed to dry out for about 10 or 15 minutes. It is now ready for use. Store your tack rag in an air-tight container when not in use to prevent it from drying out completely.

SEQUENCE OF EVENTS

The importance of a meticulous approach to creating an ultra-smooth surface prior to staining cannot be overestimated, as even apparently insignificant blemishes will mar the final effect. Refer to Chapter 3 for the appropriate methods and abrasives, and use shellac beaumontage to fill deep dents and cracks. Wherever possible, take the work apart and treat each piece as a separate item.

If you want to stain, avoid using spirit dyes, as the solvent for stain and polish is the same (alcohol), and you run the risk of lifting the colour as you polish. Remember to follow the grain-raising procedure if you water-stain (see Chapters 3 and 4).

After staining, the sequence of events is as follows.

GRAINFILLING
AND OILING

The secret of French polishing is that the polish is applied as a series of thin layers. Open-textured timbers will draw the polish straight into the fibres; the pores will remain open unless they are filled, and so a mirror finish is difficult to achieve. Filling the grain with a solid material reduces the suction and provides a uniform surface upon which to build the substantial body of polish that is needed (solid grainfiller is not suitable for carvings and mouldings, which are filled with oil; see 'Polishing awkward areas' on page 81). In some instances you may wish to keep an open-grained effect, in which case grainfilling is omitted. Oak looks particularly good when given this treatment as it retains its tactile texture. However, you will not create a mirror finish without grainfilling, and its omission is best reserved for finishes where you wish to retain an open texture and not a very high gloss.

Begin by partially sealing the wood with a brush coat of thinned French polish in a ratio of three parts polish to one part methylated spirit. Apply it quickly and thinly with a polisher's mop. This is a very soft-haired brush, with goat or squirrel hair, or a combination of hair called zorino – the latter being the most useful kind – quill-bound

to the handle (see Fig 6.4). Avoid creating runs and ridges which are very difficult to eliminate. Allow to dry overnight.

Once dry, filling may begin. Proprietary brands of grainfiller are available and should be applied according to the manufacturer's instructions. However, it is cheaper, and more traditional, to make your own.

Plaster of Paris is the traditional material, rubbed into the pores of the wood with hessian, an open-weave canvas. Place a quantity of dry plaster into a wide container, and have ready a separate container of water.

The whiteness of the plaster has to be 'killed' by mixing it with a small amount of powder pigment. The colour of the pigment should correspond to the wood (e.g. burnt sienna for reddish surfaces, burnt umber for brownish surfaces, yellow ochre for golden colours; see

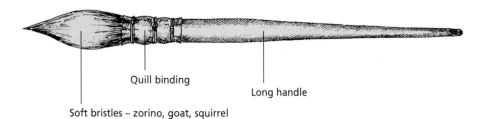

Quill binding

Long handle

Soft bristles – zorino, goat, squirrel

Fig 6.4 Polisher's mop.

Chapters 4 and 8 for more detail on pigments).

Mix in enough pigment to take off the extreme whiteness of the plaster. Then soak a piece of hessian in water and squeeze it out until it is only damp. Fold it into a pad and dip the face into the dry plaster. Transfer the plaster it picks up on to the wood, and, working a small area, say 12in (305mm) square, rub the plaster into the pores with a circular motion, using a fair amount of pressure. The plaster should form a soft paste, also known as a 'slurry'. Before it begins to set, rub off the surplus across the grain (see Fig 6.5). Never allow any surplus to remain, as it will be impossible to remove without damaging the surface once it has set. Pay particular attention to adjoining mouldings or carvings where it is difficult to avoid filler encroaching into angles. Any accumulation must be removed, and this is best achieved using matchsticks or cocktail sticks, and they will not mark the wood itself.

Repeat this process over the whole work, sectioning it off in small areas. Do not be tempted to cover a large area at once, as the plaster will harden while you are applying it. Allow the filled surfaces to dry and harden overnight.

As the work dries the pores in the grain will show up as white flecks, with a powdery residue on the surface, but there should be no solid build-up. After overnight drying the surface must be cleared of this residue and the whiteness in the pores 'killed'. Rub in enough raw linseed oil to restore the original colour, but no more; too much oil will lie on the surface and might bleed through the polish later. Rub off across the grain and leave to dry overnight. Even if the grain has not been filled, you should still carry out this oiling process as it enhances the figure.

FADDING

The wood's natural suction should now have been satisfied and a smooth ground achieved on which to apply the successive layers of burnished French polish. The polish is applied with a fad.

Give the work a good rub-over with a clean, lint-free cloth to remove residual oil and filler. Make up a fad and charge it with polish in the following way: pour the polish into a wide container such as an old cereal bowl or cleaned-out margarine tub. Dip the face of the fad into the polish, squeeze out the surplus, and distribute the remaining polish throughout the wadding by pressing the face against the edge of the container (see Fig 6.6).

GRAIN FILLING

Fig 6.5(a) Rub the plaster into the pores with a circular motion.

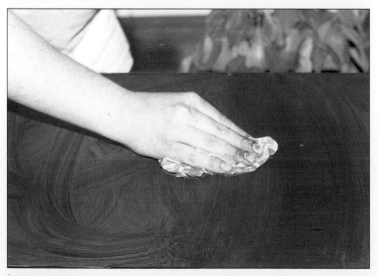

Fig 6.5(b) Rub excess plaster off the wood, across the grain.

Fig 6.6(a) Charging a fad with polish.

Fig 6.6(b) Squeezing out the surplus.

How much polish?

The fad should be charged with enough polish to create a definite streak on the work, but not so much that the polish pours out and leaves puddles. Recharge when it has dried out to the point where it becomes difficult to put polish on the surface and a uniform streak cannot be laid down.

How much pressure?

Only apply enough pressure to allow the polish to flow on to the surface. The streak of polish should be touch-dry very quickly – in seconds rather than minutes. If the film remains wet you have either used too much pressure or the fad was over-charged with polish. As the fad dries out you will need to increase the pressure until it is time to recharge, as above.

What if the fad sticks to the surface?

If this happens, reduce the pressure on the fad and you should be able to continue. If the fad begins to break up, leaving fibres sticking to the polished surface, you must stop. Wait for an hour for the surface to dry sufficiently to allow you to gently remove the fibres with a fine abrasive before continuing. If you do not feel confident at this stage, use a fingertip of raw linseed oil on the face of the fad to lubricate its path – but only a fingertip, and only in the area causing the problem.

Remember the golden rule: always keep the fad moving when in contact with the work and if the wadding begins to break up, replace it.

Straight strokes

Using light pressure at first, apply the polish to the work in straight, slightly overlapping strokes. There should be an obvious full width streak but no ridges which will be difficult to eliminate later (see Fig 6.7).

If there are several pieces to be polished, work them in rotation, covering each piece once before returning to the first piece for the second coat. If you are only polishing one piece, wait a few minutes before applying the second and subsequent coats.

After about three coats, a sheen should be starting to appear. At this point, leave the work to dry for about 15 minutes before giving it a very light sand with a fine abrasive (320 grit), and dust off.

Once you have completed this process with all pieces, the next stages are carried out on each piece *in turn*, without interruption between each stage.

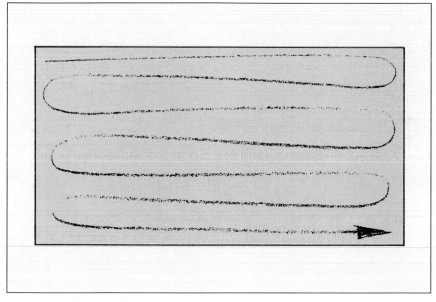

Fig 6.7 Fadding in straight strokes.

SMALL FIGURES OF EIGHT

Change the pattern of application to small figures of eight. Cover the centre of the work first, leaving a border of a couple of inches, and cover the border separately after the centre has been completed. This ensures that the edges are comprehensively fadded, as it is all too easy to miss small areas here (see Fig 6.8). If you do miss a small area, leave it until the next coat, as going over it at this point is likely to result in the fad sticking to the surface, leaving bits of itself stuck on the polish – a highly undesirable state of affairs!

LARGE FIGURES OF EIGHT

Immediately apply a second coat in large figures of eight (see Fig 6.9), in order to eliminate the circular tracks left by the fad before they dry in. Provided the fad is not too wet it should not stick. Any small areas missed during the small figures of eight phase are covered at this stage.

STRAIGHT STROKES

Finish off by applying straight strokes along the grain. Do not overlap them, as this will lead to sticking. Guide the fad on to one end and off the other, as shown in Fig 6.10.

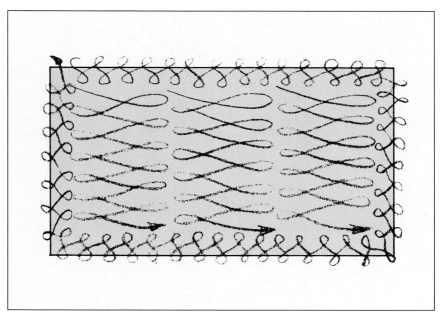

Fig 6.8 Small figures of eight.

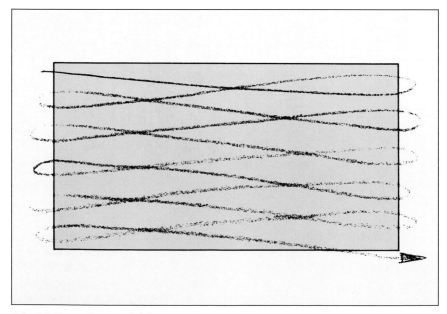

Fig 6.9 Large figures of eight.

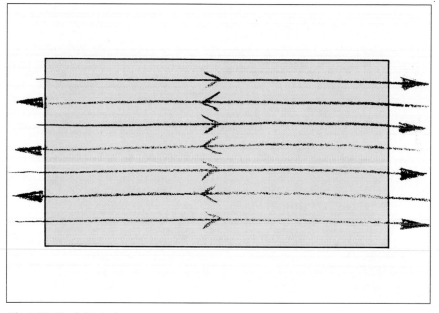

Fig 6.10 Straight strokes.

The straight strokes should be just that; avoid arcing the stroke, which is the natural sweep of the arm movement. For long surfaces such as dining tables, it may not be possible to complete each stroke in one movement. In such cases, start the stroke at one end and 'glide' the fad off the surface at the midpoint. Cover one half like this and then repeat with the other half. The area in the centre where the strokes meet may show slight marking but this will disappear as the polish dries and hardens.

Allow 15 minutes for the piece to dry before repeating the entire fadding process for a second coat. At this stage the quality of the finish will not be anything to write home about, but should have a shine, perhaps with a few dull areas where the fad has dragged, which is only to be expected. If the grain has been filled there should be little evidence of the pores, and the surface should be fairly smooth. With luck it will be completely free of adhering pieces of fad, friction marks, or ridges!

Now allow the polish to harden overnight. After this you will find that the film of polish has shrunk and some sinking into the wood will be evident. This is quite normal and is one of the main reasons for allowing a long drying period.

You must now cut back the fadded film of polish, to create a flawless, smooth ground on which to build a deep, lustrous film. Cut back with 320 grit abrasive, using only sufficient pressure to dislodge adhering particles of dust and fibres of wadding and create a uniform dullness over the surface with no high spots or ridges. Dust off regularly, and use your fingertips to feel for any blemishes. Take great care not to cut through the film of shellac. Should this happen, restain the bare patch, allow to dry and then apply polish to the area very carefully with a polisher's mop. When dry, gently cut back.

COLOUR CORRECTION

It is often the case that when you begin polishing, the colour of the work is not right; perhaps it is too red or too green in hue, or the overall colour balance is right but too light. If it is too dark, there is nothing to be done other than strip the work and start again! It is only *after* fadding that such discrepancies can be seen with any degree of certainty, and the process of colour correction begun.

Chapter 8 explains the process of colouring and advises which colour to use. The general principle involves putting colour into the polish itself and applying it with a rubber, using the same technique as fadding. Most colour errors can, thankfully, be corrected without stripping, and colour is added to the polish because the wood cannot now be stained, having been sealed during fadding.

If you have had to apply corrective layers of coloured polish, allow the work to harden off for a few hours before sealing in the colour with a couple of coats of French polish, applied in straight strokes with a rubber. Allow to dry overnight before proceeding to the bodying stage.

BODYING

If you have stored the fad properly, as described on page 57, it should contain enough polish to use as a rubber without recharging. At the same time, it will have been broken in and its shape established. Convert the fad to a rubber, as described on page 57.

Fig 6.11 shows how the rubber should be charged. Open up the wadding and pour in a small quantity of polish from a bottle. Test for the quantity of polish by pressing the rubber against a sheet of clean, white paper. Fig 6.12 shows the results of too little, too much and the right amount of polish. If you have applied too much polish open up the wadding

Fig 6.11 Charging a rubber.

and allow it to dry out for a while before retesting and, if necessary, recharging.

Overcharging will cause ridges that cannot be removed easily, and an excessive flow on the surface will cause the rubber to stick or 'burn' the previous layers of shellac.

You may come across the method of using raw linseed oil as a lubricant for the face of the rubber to prevent it sticking to the soft, newly applied polish. I have found this creates more problems than it solves, as the oil has to be taken off again, and any residual oil may bleed through later, causing dullness. The oil also attracts moisture from the atmosphere, increasing the risk of blooming. If care is exercised there should be no need for oil, except on problem areas if you are not confident enough to continue, as described on page 68.

Hold the rubber as shown in Fig 6.3(b), and body the work following the steps shown below. Keep the wrist firm, and try to activate the rubber's movement from the elbow or shoulder.

SMALL FIGURES OF EIGHT

Body the centre of the work with small figures of eight as you did

HOW MUCH POLISH?

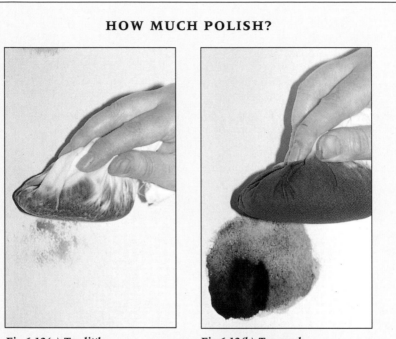

Fig 6.12(a) Too little.   *Fig 6.12(b) Too much.*

Fig 6.12(c) The correct amount.

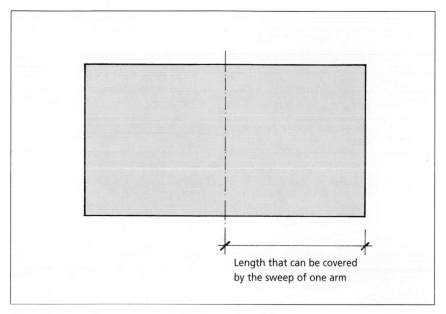

Length that can be covered
by the sweep of one arm

*Fig 6.13 It may be necessary to divide the work up into two or three sections if the
length is too great to cover in one sweep.*

with the fad (see Fig 6.8), and then
work around the edge until the
whole piece is covered. If the rubber
is too wet, stop, allow the surface to
dry for an hour or so before gently
cutting back with 320 grit abrasive.

LARGE FIGURES OF EIGHT

Immediately proceed to working
large overlapping figures of eight
along the grain over the whole
surface, as shown in Fig 6.9. Once
again if the work is too long to be
covered in one sweep, divide it into
sections (see Fig 6.13).

By this stage you should be
experiencing some resistance to the
motion of the rubber. The best way
to experience the amount of pull
required is to simulate the
movement of the rubber by rubbing
the ball of your hand (the fleshy bit
below the thumb) over the surface
of a clean window pane. Apply only
enough pressure on the rubber to
deposit the polish and achieve this
amount of pull. Excessive pressure
will lead to tearing up, but some
friction is needed to pull the polish
flat as it is deposited on the surface.

Increased pressure will be
required as the rubber dries, and
recharging will be necessary when
the face of the rubber feels warm
when tested against the back of

your hand. If it feels cold and moist there is probably enough polish to continue. If you still experience problems, such as excessive drag, or no drag at all, change the rag, as it is probably clogged. The rag should also be changed if you can see tiny scratch marks or hear the sound of grit under the rubber.

STRAIGHT STROKES

Finally, to eliminate the path marks of the figures of eight, work along the grain with slightly overlapping straight strokes, gliding on and off the edges. If swirls remain, repeat the process once or twice, but take extra care with the pressure you apply as the risk of sticking is increased. It may be better to recharge the rubber and use less pressure; experience will tell you the best course of action to take.

When all the pieces have received a full body, allow about 15 minutes' drying time before applying another coat. The pull on the rubber will now increase; exercise care to avoid tearing up the soft polish. Keep the rubber movement deliberate, well controlled, and slow enough to achieve good results without sticking.

The number of coats depends upon the type of finish you desire. Continue bodying until you achieve a good, deep sheen, or until the rubber is determined to stick to the work. Leave to dry and harden overnight, when, as with fadding, the film of polish will shrink a little. The following day, if you want a deeper body, cut back with 400 or 600 grit silicon carbide paper (wet-or-dry) or a piece of very fine nylon pad abrasive, so as to remove surface blemishes like rubber marks or dust, before bodying up again. The minimum number of coats, or bodies, is usually three or four, but for a mirror finish you will need more, and burnishing will also be required; see page 78. You must use your own judgement in relation to the type of finish you wish to achieve.

Immediately after each body you may see minor rubber marks; do not worry – these should disappear as the polish hardens.

STIFFING OR SPIRITING

In most cases this is the final stage, designed to burnish the polish to a high gloss. *Do not* use pure methylated spirit in a rubber for this process, as the powerful solvent action will probably burn up the polish, ruining your work. Use French polish thinned down with a little methylated spirit, in a ratio of three parts polish to one part methylated spirit.

Make up a new rubber, reserved for stiffing only, and store it

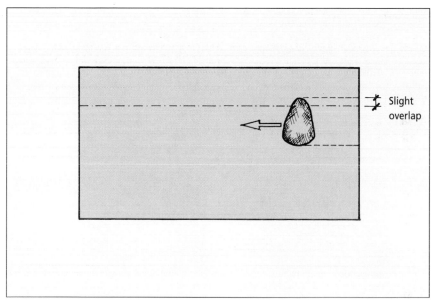

Slight overlap

Fig 6.14 Stiffing, using very slightly overlapping strokes.

separately from your bodying rubbers. After the polish has hardened overnight, cut back the film very slightly with a very fine grit. An abrasive-impregnated nylon pad in a very fine grade is ideal for this, as you only need to gently rub away imperfections, and no more.

Now charge the stiffing rubber with the polish mixture and proceed, using very light pressure, as though you were applying another body, finishing off with the straight and slightly overlapping strokes (see Fig 6.14). When all the pieces have been treated in this way, wait a few minutes and then repeat. This time you should experience a very definite pull (hence the term

'stiffing'), as the surface film is partially dissolved, and pulled flat by the rubber. Two or three coats, with a few minutes in between each, should be enough. If you experience any difficulties, stop, as always, for about an hour, and then begin again.

The work should now be allowed to harden overnight, and all remaining blemishes such as rubber marks should disappear as the polish hardens. If they do not, the stiffing process should be repeated.

Further finishing techniques can be applied after stiffing to achieve different effects, although stiffing produces a very fine finish in itself.

BURNISHING

This will produce the classic mirror finish! A very deep body of polish is needed to make it effective, and grain filler must have been used at the beginning of the process. Do not attempt to burnish an open-grained finish as the burnishing cream will collect in the pores and turn them white.

After stiffing, allow the work to harden for at least a day in a warm environment. Use a proprietary burnishing cream, pour a little on to a damp polishing cloth, and quickly distribute it evenly over the whole surface, using straight strokes along the grain and only slight pressure (see Fig 6.15). Wait for the cream to dry fully before wiping it off along the grain with a soft, dry polishing cloth. The process can be repeated if a full mirror gloss has not been achieved, and any residual haze can be removed using a reviver. See Chapter 9 for information on using revivers, and Chapter 12 for recipes.

DULLING

If on the other hand the high gloss left by stiffing is too great, it can be dulled down using one of two methods: dulling with pumice powder and a soft brush, or, more commonly, dulling with steel wool and wax polish.

Fig 6.15 Distributing burnishing cream over a French polished surface.

PUMICE POWDER

This is lightly dusted over the hardened polish using a pounce bag made from a square of open-weave cotton. A tablespoon of pumice powder is placed in the centre of the square, and the corners are brought up and tied, as shown in Fig 6.16. When gently shaken up and down about 12in (305mm) over the work, the bag will lightly dust the surface with pumice powder. The idea is to give a light and even dusting over the entire surface. A soft-haired brush is then run along the grain in slightly overlapping strokes, creating tiny scratches which run along the grain direction and so reduce the gloss (see Fig 6.17). The amount of dulling is controlled by the pressure applied and the number of times you brush over the work.

When you have finished, *do not wipe off the dust:* blow it off, as wiping will create obvious scratches

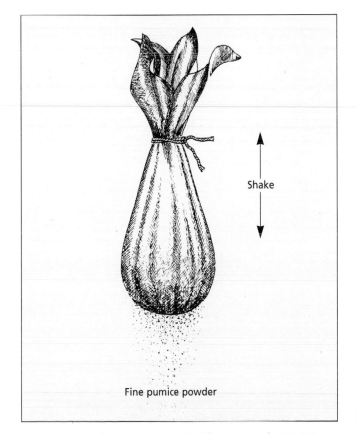

Shake

Fine pumice powder

Fig 6.16 The pounce bag.

Fig 6.17 Dulling with pumice and a soft brush.

across the grain. Finally, wipe away any remaining particles along the grain with a tack rag, using no pressure.

STEEL WOOL

This is the easiest and most common way of dulling a gloss finish. Its effect is to reduce the gloss while giving the polish the look of having been hand-buffed for many years.

Use the finest grades of steel wool (000 or 0000). Make up a generous sized pad of wool, dip it into a wax polish paste and rub the pad over the work in full-length strokes along the grain (see Fig 6.18). Renew the wax as the pad works dry, but do not be too heavy-handed with the amount of wax used, or you will have a terrible job trying to remove it all at the buffing stage.

Again, the amount of dulling is determined by the pressure you apply and the number of times you rub over the work. When finished, allow the wax polish to dry, and buff with a warmed polishing cloth (the heat helps to distribute the polished wax).

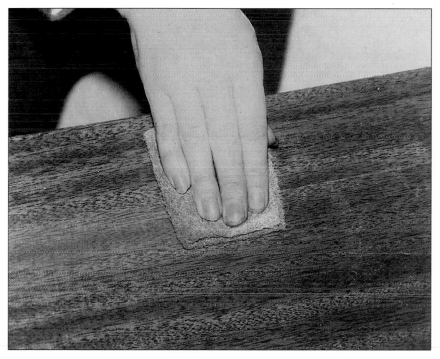

Fig 6.18 Dulling with steel wool and wax polish.

POLISHING AWKWARD AREAS

As I mentioned in the section on grainfilling, many items will have areas that are inaccessible to a fad or rubber, such as carvings, mouldings and small corners. For these you should use a polisher's mop and squirrel pencil brushes (see Fig 6.19).

CARVINGS AND MOULDINGS

Use the polisher's mop to apply polish in both the fadding and bodying stages. Stiffing is not possible. Apply thinly to avoid runs and drips. On carvings, work the polish well into the crevices and undercuts. It is possible to burnish or dull mouldings, but carvings are not normally subjected to these processes.

CORNERS

Even a well-made fad or rubber cannot reach right into all the angles, which are left dry. Use a squirrel pencil brush to apply polish to these areas.

Fig 6.19 A pencil brush being used to apply polish in crevices and sharp angles.

POLISHING FAULTS

There are three main things which can go wrong during the process of French polishing:

BLOOM

The polish will go dull, and may show milkiness during application in a cold or damp environment, or if a draught is blowing directly on to the surface. If the problem is not too great you can cut back affected areas after allowing time to harden, adjust the environment to suitable conditions if necessary, and recommence polishing. In serious cases you may have to strip the work and start again.

RUBBER BURNS

As mentioned before, these are caused by too much pressure or too wet a rubber. The symptoms are dullness and, in bad cases, a degree of roughness. Allow the work to harden, cut back, and polish again.

FINGERPRINTING

If the work is handled too soon after polishing, it may show the impressions of fingers and hands, even though it appears hard. Again, allow to harden, cut back and repolish.

7
VARNISHING

The basic formulation of varnishes has not fundamentally changed over the centuries in terms of general principles, although the materials have become increasingly sophisticated. Varnish is classified as any solution of a gum or resin in a solvent, which dries to produce a hard, transparent finish.

TYPES OF VARNISH

POLYURETHANE

Heralded during the 1960s as a significant breakthrough in paint and varnish technology, this polymer was marketed on the basis of its extreme hardness and durability.

In fact, these very properties are also its source of weakness: the fact that it is brittle. Polyurethane is not very elastic, and if subjected to conditions in which expansion and contraction of the piece takes place regularly (such as the exterior door featured in Chapter 1, Fig 1.1), the film will ultimately crack and flake away. It follows from this that polyurethane is more suited to interior use. There are specially formulated polyurethane varnishes for exterior use, but they still do not have the durability of alkyd resin.

Even indoors, polyurethane can be subject to adverse conditions: window boards are subject to condensation running on to them from the window glass, as well as heat from the sun. Fluctuations in the moisture levels within the wood, along with expansion and contraction due to temperature changes, will cause rapid breakdown of the varnish film.

These are classic examples of a very good product being used in inappropriate situations. In most interior environments, polyurethane provides a highly durable finish and a mechanical resistance to wear and tear.

ALKYD RESIN

This material is the basis of the external varnishes, frequently referred to as 'yacht' or 'marine' varnish. These are heavy-bodied varnishes which require longer drying periods than polyurethane. If brushed on too thickly they easily 'sag' (wrinkle), and take forever to dry. They are less brittle than polyurethane, and so will move with the wood to some degree. They are also more resistant to corrosive chemical attack, hence their use in marine environments due to their resistance to salt corrosion.

Coloured varnishes, which are based on alkyd resins, contain UV-absorbing pigments to protect the wood from harmful UV rays.

ACRYLIC VARNISHES

The current preoccupation with developing solvent-free products has yielded these water-based varnishes, which are a welcome addition to the marketplace. There is even a specially formulated acrylic/polyurethane blend for use on floors.

Since water-based products dry very quickly compared with traditional drying times, the convenience factor alone makes these varnishes a good investment. A two-hour drying time, for example, enables a three-coat varnishing job to be completed in a single day!

MICROPOROUS VARNISHES

Technically speaking these varnishes are described as 'moisture vapour permeable' (MVP). They are able to tolerate what to other varnishes would be an unacceptable level of moisture in the wood (providing it is not actually wet). Normally, as trapped moisture evaporates and tries to escape it will cause the

varnish to crack and peel. MVPs on the other hand allow the vapour to escape through the varnish film (provided it is not too thick), but at the same time provide a barrier against rain. In effect, MVPs allow the wood to 'breathe' (see Fig 7.1). If you combine this property with preservatives and UV filtering pigments, you have the basis of an extremely useful exterior grade varnish, which is also extremely suited to use in high humidity indoor environments such as kitchens and bathrooms.

MVP products, if properly applied, will generally last longer than alkyd varnishes, but must of course be applied to unfinished surfaces, not on top of other, non-MVP varnishes!

Most MVPs are solvent-based, but the latest generation of exterior varnishes is water-based.

FINISHES AND STAINS

FINISHES

Varnishes can be obtained in clear (uncoloured), pigmented (stain varnishes), matt, satin (eggshell) or gloss finishes. The choice of finish is one of personal preference, but many internal surfaces look better with a satin rather than a full gloss finish. This is particularly the case with large areas such as panelling.

MVP VARNISH

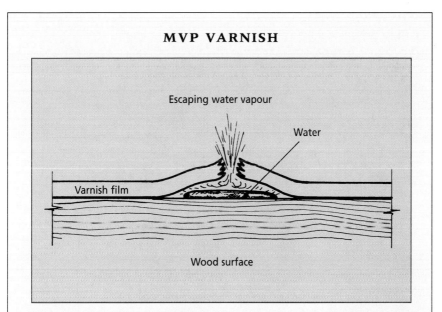

Fig 7.1(a) *Non-MVP varnish blisters as water vapour tries to escape.*

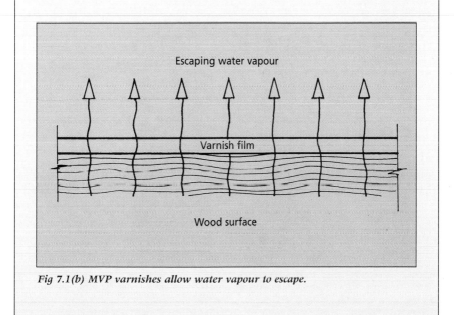

Fig 7.1(b) *MVP varnishes allow water vapour to escape.*

The reflective surface of gloss can diminish the effect of the wood's figure, and can result in an unattractive, treacly finish unless you pay meticulous attention to the surface preparation and varnish application. This highlights what I said in Chapter 1 about planning and asking yourself pertinent questions about your project well in advance.

STAINS

Varnish stains have several advantages over using a stain followed by a clear varnish: you save time, and, because they are heavy-bodied, they do not become absorbed too deeply in the wood. This makes them ideal for woods of variable absorbency, which would otherwise lead to patchy staining. Varnish stains will produce a more even colour, but they do cloud the surface, especially the darker colours due to their heavy pigment. As a result the figure of the wood becomes obscured if you apply more than one coat. You can compromise by using one coat of pigmented varnish, followed by clear top coats.

EXTERIOR VARNISH 'SYSTEMS'

Several manufacturers produce 'systems', i.e. two or more coating materials designed to be used in conjunction with each other. They are designed for exterior use, and meet stringent architects' specifications, for which they were originally developed. They incorporate a means of preserving the wood as well as colouring and varnishing, and usually comprise a first coat preservative, and top coats of coloured protective varnishes (usually referred to as woodstains). The first preserving coat will protect the wood for a given period, and so can be factory-applied, making the wood safe until final finishing can take place. For this reason it is a very commonly used system in the building trade, and all major paint and varnish manufacturers have their own products of this type.

VARNISH BRUSHES

Reserve a special set of brushes for varnishing, and never use a brush which has been used for painting; varnish can be contaminated by specks of paint. As ever, the best results are more easily obtained by using the best tools. Traditional varnish brushes are oval in cross-section, which allows the bristles to flow around edges and mouldings (see Fig 7.2). Cheap brushes are never worthwhile as they always drop their bristles in the varnish film.

Fig 7.2 An oval varnish brush. This one has been well used but also well looked after, and will last many more years, representing an extremely good investment.

If you have spent good money on a brush you will want to keep it in good condition. When you have finished varnishing, clean the brush several times in white spirit, and a final time in a proprietary brush cleaner, rinsing it out in cold water. For water-based varnish, warm water is all that is required to clean the brush.

If you are not intending to use the brush in the near future, wrap the bristles in brown paper as shown in Fig 7.3 and store the brush in such a way that the bristles do not become bent.

Do not clean the brush between coats, as the bristles become more pliable and softer with use, producing a better finish. It is important to keep the bristles wet

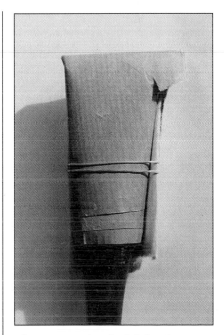

Fig 7.3 Protecting the bristles of a varnish brush before storing for future use.

between coats, and for this you will need a glass container filled with keeper varnish. This is varnish thinned to the ratio of three parts varnish to one part white spirit. Do not use turpentine alone, as this will cause the varnish to run when you begin the next coat. Keep the brush suspended in keeper varnish so that the bristles do not touch the bottom of the container; a nail or other suitable piece of metal through a hole in the brush handle is a very effective method of achieving this (see Fig 7.4). Use a clean lint-free rag to remove surplus keeper varnish before beginning the next coat.

SURFACE PREPARATION

Always ensure the wood is dry before commencing. Prepare the

Fig 7.4 Temporary brush storage between coats in keeper varnish, ensuring the bristles do not make contact with the bottom of the jar.

work in the usual way, paying particular attention to eliminating dust with a tack rag. As solvent-based varnishes are generally slow-drying, they will readily pick up dust.

Previously varnished surfaces that are sound, i.e. not peeling, may be recoated without stripping, but must first be washed down with water and mild detergent, allowed to dry and then 'keyed' by rubbing down with fine abrasive paper.

The surface must be stripped if it is peeling, and also if you intend to use an MVP varnish and the old varnish is not MVP, even if the surface is sound.

Remember: if the work is being stained, water-based stains will be compatible but oil stains may not, due to the risk of lifting the stain when applying the varnish, resulting in patchiness. You can apply a coat of transparent French polish as an isolating barrier between stain and varnish, but not in the case of MVP varnishes or exterior work, as the shellac will not allow vapour to escape.

THE VARNISHING ENVIRONMENT

It is not always possible to operate in ideal conditions, especially with exterior work, and you can expect to have to compromise to some extent. The best conditions for varnishing are:

- A warm dry atmosphere to aid drying, avoiding direct sunlight. For exterior work, this limits working times to spring and summer. Begin and finish work as early as possible to allow maximum drying time before the chill and damp of night.
- A dust-free atmosphere! Although this is impossible, reduce any disturbance of settled dust. This means not moving anything (if at all possible), and certainly means no woodwork in the workshop at the same time as varnishing! Constant use of the tack rag before varnishing surfaces is important, because you can't always see the dust until the varnish is applied. If there is a dust-lifting breeze, don't varnish.

APPLYING THE VARNISH

Whatever type of varnish you're using, the basic rules are the same:

- Make sure all tools and surfaces are absolutely clean.
- Adhere strictly to the drying times recommended by the manufacturer.
- Apply several thin coats rather than one thick.

NEW, PREVIOUSLY UNFINISHED, OR STRIPPED SURFACES

These will be rather absorbent, so thin the first coat of varnish with 10% white spirit (water in the case of acrylics) by volume. Apply fairly generously, avoiding runs, and remove any brush bristles that find their way on to the work as soon as you notice them; never allow them to dry in.

When thoroughly dry, denib with 240 grit abrasive, taking care not to cut through to the wood, then tack rag the surface clean of dust. Apply subsequent coats unthinned, and cut back each coat with 600 grit wet-or-dry, using water with a little detergent as a lubricant. Dry and tack rag before applying the next coat. Do not cut back the final coat unless you intend to burnish or dull the finish (see 'Alternative finishes' on page 92).

The number of coats depends upon the circumstances: in general, the more wear expected or the more adverse the conditions, the more coats will be required. The exception to this is MVP, where no more than three coats are applied; any more than this diminishes the microporosity.

Apply two or three coats to furniture, at least four to floors (more in heavy traffic areas), and four coats of yacht varnish on external woodwork. If you intend to burnish to a high gloss, apply an extra coat (not applicable to MVP).

OLD, SOUND VARNISHED SURFACES

Wash these down with water and a little detergent, and allow to dry. Provide a key by rubbing down well with 240 grit abrasive, and tack rag clean of dust. The work is now ready to receive two coats of varnish (one if MVP), with wet-or-dry treatment between them.

BRUSHING TECHNIQUE

Brush technique goes a long way to producing a good finish. Narrow-sectioned timber such as legs and rails has the varnish brushed along the grain, while larger areas such as table tops, panels and floors require a different technique to ensure every portion is covered.

Charge the brush with varnish to two-thirds of the bristle length, and squeeze the tips against the side of the container. Varnish large areas in sections, each of a size capable of being covered by about two or three brush loads. First brush the varnish along the grain, then across it. Finally, draw the bristle tips very lightly along the grain in straight strokes to eliminate brushstrokes.

BRUSHING ON VARNISH

1	2	3
4	5	6
7	8	9

Fig 7.5(a) Sectioning off the work for large areas.

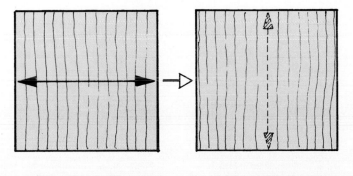

Fig 7.5(b) First apply the varnish against the grain.

Fig 7.5(c) Apply finishing strokes along the grain.

Then move on to the next section until the whole surface is covered. Allow each section to overlap slightly, ensuring there are no 'dry' areas. Fig 7.5 illustrates this approach, with the arrows showing the direction of the finishing strokes in relation to the grain. Fig 7.6 shows the order of varnishing for panelled work.

ALTERNATIVE FINISHES

You can burnish varnished surfaces to a mirror gloss, or dull them to a semi- or full matt, although it is easier to use satin or matt varnishes to achieve this effect. In all cases the varnish should be allowed to harden for as long as possible – at least 48 hours for polyurethane, and up to a week for yacht varnish.

BURNISHING

Make sure the surface is perfectly flat and free of all blemishes such as dust specks and brush marks. Cut back the varnish film with 600 grit wet-or-dry with water and detergent, until all blemishes have been removed and there are no bright, glossy areas. Wipe, allow to dry and then tack rag.

Special burnishing creams are available, but 'T-Cut' or a similar abrasive fluid – even metal polish – will do. Slightly dampen a pad of stockinette large enough to fit into the palm of your hand, and spread enough cream over its face to cover the work. Distribute the cream over the surface without any pressure, and then apply pressure in circular motions over the whole surface until the shine returns, remembering not to linger in any one area for too long. Finally, apply pressure, working along the grain. Clean off the cream with a clean cloth, allow to dry and then buff, along the grain. A haze may remain, but this can be removed with a reviver (see Chapter 12).

A surface in which the pores of the wood can be seen should not be burnished, as the cream will accumulate in the small cavities, leaving an unsightly white deposit which is difficult to remove. If necessary, apply more coats of varnish to achieve full grain condition.

DULLING

A gloss finish can be dulled down to a full matt by gently rubbing along the grain with 0000 wire wool – the very tiny scratches caused by the wool destroy the gloss. If you still want a sheen, but dislike the high 'plastic' gloss that a varnish can sometimes give, lubricate the wire wool with some furniture wax. Do not use too much, otherwise you will end up with a greasy surface.

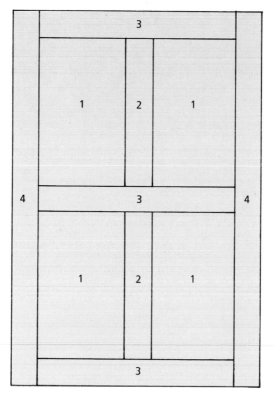

Fig 7.6 Order of varnishing panelled work.

Then buff when the wax has dried, which usually takes about an hour. You can vary the degree of dulling by using different grades of wire wool with wax polish: 0000 wool with a light pressure will produce an almost burnished sheen, while 0 will produce significant dulling.

VARNISHING FLOORS

The main properties of a varnish designed for finishing floors are extreme durability and rapid drying time, allowing recoating within as short a period as possible. This reduces the amount of dust fallout from the air that becomes trapped within the surface – especially important if a high gloss is required.

Most manufacturers produce a floor varnish, which should be used in preference to ordinary varnishes. All floor varnishes are based on relatively fast-drying solvents and polymers. One or two require an extended period when the floor cannot be used, to allow time for the varnish to harden, or cure, by chemical action. Such varnishes will produce very tough finishes but may be rather inconvenient. At the other end of the scale, there are water-based (acrylic) floor varnishes that are very fast-drying and allow you to recoat within a couple of hours. In theory, you could finish a job the same day – ideal for areas which are in constant use.

You may have to compromise to a degree, in that a traffic lane has sometimes to be kept open. Varnish the rest of the floor, and work on the area left clear once the rest has hardened sufficiently to use. The only drawback here is the possibility of colour-matching problems, if you are staining.

The greatest embarrassment comes when you trap yourself in a room surrounded by wet varnished floor. (Believe it or not, this does happen!) Always plan your varnishing so that you start at the point furthest away from the entrance/exit, and finish at the point where you can escape (see Fig 7.7). Ensure there is some ventilation, but do not leave windows wide open, otherwise you will invite dust, leaves and other windblown material to take up permanent residence. Always close the room off afterwards, to prevent roaming animals and humans increasing your blood pressure.

Heat in the room will aid drying, but do not overheat, as the varnish will go tacky while you are applying it. Around 20°C is quite enough. As I mentioned earlier, four coats is about right, but you might need more in very well-trodden areas. If you have the time and the patience, gently hand-sand between coats.

CORK AND
PARQUET FLOORS

After laying a cork or parquet floor, some time must elapse to allow the adhesive to dry, and its solvent to evaporate off. A couple of days should be enough. Instructions for laying these floors include the procedure for cleaning off adhesive from the surface.

Always brush and vacuum clean the floor prior to varnishing to remove dust and any other loose material. The first coat can be thinned with the appropriate solvent, up to 10%. Apply subsequent coats unthinned. Floors tend to look better if they are varnished matt or semi-matt; such a finish is also less slippery. Any runners or mats laid on the floor should be made non-slip in any case, using one of the many non-slip products available for this purpose.

Cork floors should never be sanded, as the material is rather

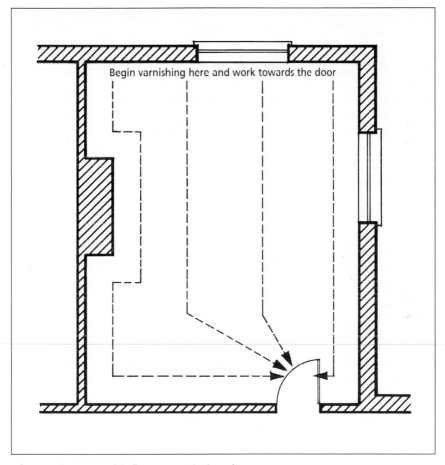

Begin varnishing here and work towards the door

Fig 7.7 Always varnish floors towards the exit.

thin, but parquet can be machine-sanded. Always use a belt sander with a medium belt, followed by a fine belt (see Chapter 2). Vacuum clean the floor afterwards to remove as much dust as possible, and allow a couple of days or so for the airborne dust to settle before vacuuming again prior to varnishing.

FLOORBOARDS

Fill the gaps between old floorboards with wedges of wood. This is for two reasons:

- The gaps are a source of draughts.
- Small objects and liquids may fall into the cavity below.

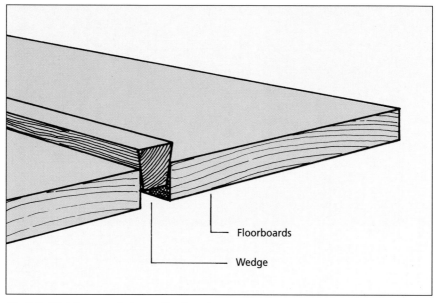

Fig 7.8 Wedging gaps between floorboards.

Fig 7.8 shows how the gaps are wedged. They should be left proud until the glue has dried, and then planed flush. The boards can be sanded and stained afterwards, if required.

MAINTENANCE

Maintaining a varnished floor is not difficult, although dressing it with wax is not recommended! Nothing more than damp dusting is needed, unless the floor is heavily soiled. As soon as any wear begins to show, wash the floor, sand it lightly to create a key, and apply a couple of coats of varnish. If a floor is allowed to deteriorate too much, you may have no option other than to strip and varnish all over again – hence it pays to attack wear as it becomes noticeable.

A traditional recipe for reviving 'tired' floors is a 50/50 mixture of white vinegar and paraffin. Shake the mixture to emulsify it and apply sparingly with a cloth, finally buffing to bring up the finish.

VARNISHING FAULTS

Most varnishing problems arise because of poor environmental conditions, inadequate preparation or careless application. Commonly occurring faults are:

NIBS

These are adhering particles which have become trapped in the varnish film. To a degree they are unavoidable because of the extended drying time of solvent-based varnishes, but they can be reduced. Adequate sanding between coats prevents the cumulative effect of new particles being added to the previous crop. This and careful dusting down with a tack rag are essential practices. Nibs are most disfiguring on gloss finishes, and can be removed using the burnishing technique described above.

TACKINESS

If a varnish film is still tacky after the recommended drying time, the following may be the causes:

- A cold or damp working environment, which inhibits evaporation of solvent from the film, and prevents the remaining 'solid' component from hardening as well.
- Heavy coating, especially with heavy-bodied varnishes such as yacht varnish. The problem here is that the film of varnish 'skins' over: the surface dries, trapping wet varnish beneath it, and the solvent can now only escape very slowly, causing an extension of drying time.
- The varnish itself is too old. Old varnish may have deteriorated to a point where it will not dry properly because certain active ingredients responsible for speeding up the drying may have evaporated off. If you must use an old tin of varnish that has been knocking around in the cold, damp garage, then add a dash of paint drier (terebene) just in case. (Remember terebene is poisonous, so treat it with caution, both in handling and storage.)

BLOOM

Varnish applied to damp wood or in damp conditions may develop a milky, opalescent surface, caused by moisture trapped in the varnish as the solvent evaporates. In mild cases, a thorough sanding should eliminate the bloom, but in extreme cases where the film is practically white, there is no alternative but to strip and revarnish, after the wood has been allowed to dry or when environmental conditions improve.

Blooming does not always occur straight away, and may develop some months after the varnish is applied. Whenever it occurs, damp is the culprit, and if you suspect this possibility in advance, use a microporous varnish.

SAGGING

A fault found mostly on vertical or sloping surfaces, resulting from loss of adhesion between coats of varnish (see Fig 7.9). Runs and drips occur almost immediately the varnish is applied, but sagging may happen long after the varnish has apparently dried.

Loss of adhesion is caused by two things, often in combination:

- Bad surface preparation, which prevents a good bond between coats, especially if there is grease or dirt present.

- An excessively thick coat of varnish. If this is applied over a poorly finished surface, you have the perfect combination for sagging. The top coat may 'hold', and even appear to dry, but gravity may have other ideas. If the weight of the film is greater than the adhesive force holding it to the previous coat, the new coat will begin to slide off, resulting in sagging.

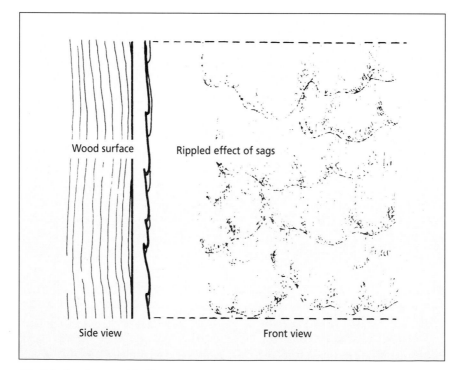

Wood surface   Rippled effect of sags

Side view   Front view

Fig 7.9 Sagging varnish film.

8
COLOURING

One of the most difficult areas of woodfinishing is colour. Sometimes the stain you apply appears to be the right colour until you start polishing. The change that takes place can be quite striking, and there are two basic reasons for this:

▌ The polish itself may be coloured, and will add its own cast to the colour of the wood.
▌ The way light is reflected from the surface can cause colour change. Polish alters light's reflective characteristics, and so seems to affect the colour of the wood.

Then again, you may simply have made a mistake! Always take the colour of the wood into account when choosing a stain, and test the colour on a piece of timber from the same batch used for the work being polished. You must also remember that wood is not a homogeneous material; it varies tremendously in terms of colour, porosity and figuring, and staining alone will not produce an even hue. This problem can be even more acute when trying to colour-match repaired patches to the original surrounding area.

Correcting a colour cast is a tricky process, and one in which you need to have a thorough understanding of how light and colour behave. For example, it is only by knowing how colours interact with each other that using a 'wash' of green stain or polish to correct a fiery red cast becomes the obvious solution.

THE COLOUR SPECTRUM AND COLOUR VISION

Most of us can distinguish between the seven colours of the spectrum with ease. However, there are those who experience difficulty in distinguishing between certain colours, and it could be said that each individual's perception of colour is just that: individual. There have been occasions when I have been aware of a difference in colour, while someone else does not seem to perceive it at all. The reverse situation has also occurred. Colouring can therefore be a contentious issue at times!

Fig 8.1 shows the colours of the spectrum as they are represented conventionally, from red through to violet. The order aids understanding of how our eyes and brains perceive colours when dyes and pigments are mixed.

Fig 8.1 The colour spectrum.

Fig 8.2(a) represents a blue-painted object. When light falls on it, some is reflected and the rest absorbed. The material reflects its own colour – blue – and absorbs all the other colours, except for a small amount of the two colours adjacent to blue in the spectrum – green and indigo. By the same principle, a yellow-painted object will reflect yellow light and absorb all the others except for a little green and orange (see Fig 8.2(b)).

Why then do we see green when we mix blue and yellow paints together? When light strikes the green object, the blue pigment will attempt to reflect its band of colours (blue, with a little indigo and green), but the yellow pigment will absorb the blue and indigo and attempt to reflect its own colour band (yellow with a little green and orange). The blue pigment will absorb yellow light and the orange. Now, all the colours have been absorbed by the object's surface bar óne – green, and this is reflected and seen by our eyes. Thus, by mixing blue and yellow we arrive at green (see Fig 8.2(c)). It is worth spending time working through and digesting the logic of this, as it will help you to understand the principles behind using some very strange colours to correct finishing errors.

THE COLOUR TRIANGLE

In theory, if all the primary colours are mixed together the result is black, because all the light would be absorbed and none would be reflected. In practice this does not happen because coloured pigments are imperfect, causing some light to be reflected, and leading to the familiar muddy hue.

You can use the colour triangle (see Fig 8.3) to work out how to correct an unwanted colour cast. The points of the triangle represent the primary colours (blue, red and yellow). The sides represent the colours produced when the primary colours are mixed, and the centre shows the result of mixing all three primary colours. A colour cast is corrected by applying the colour

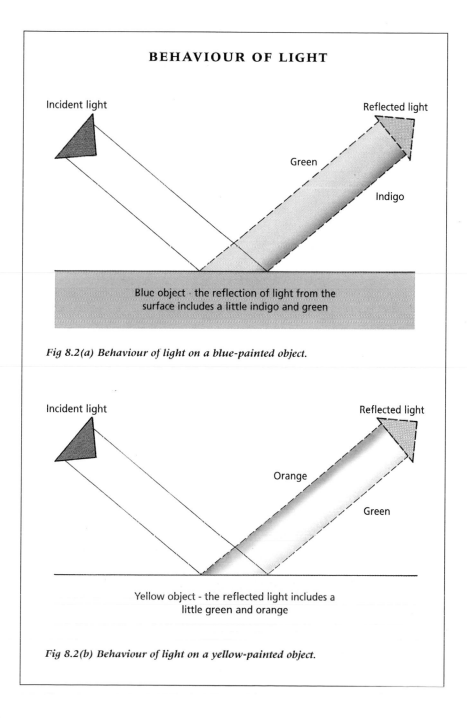

BEHAVIOUR OF LIGHT

Incident light

Reflected light

Green

Indigo

Blue object - the reflection of light from the surface includes a little indigo and green

Fig 8.2(a) Behaviour of light on a blue-painted object.

Incident light

Reflected light

Orange

Green

Yellow object - the reflected light includes a little green and orange

Fig 8.2(b) Behaviour of light on a yellow-painted object.

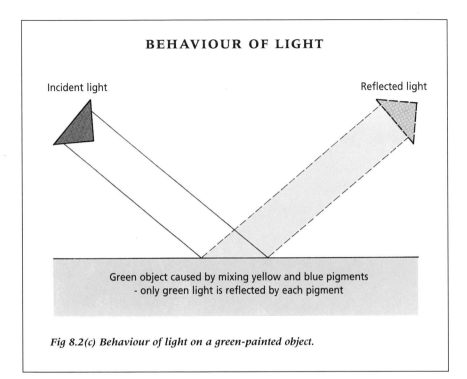

BEHAVIOUR OF LIGHT

Incident light

Reflected light

Green object caused by mixing yellow and blue pigments
- only green light is reflected by each pigment

Fig 8.2(c) Behaviour of light on a green-painted object.

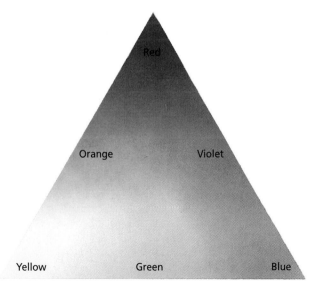

Red

Orange   Violet

Yellow   Green   Blue

Fig 8.3 The colour triangle.

opposite to it in the triangle. For example, red is neutralized by green, yellow by violet. Thus, in the case of our fiery red cast (very common when finishing mahogany, walnut or oak), consultation of the triangle shows that this can be toned down with a coat of green.

COLOUR CORRECTION

How you go about the correction process depends upon the finish concerned. Manufacturers of spray lacquers produce toning colours which can be mixed with the lacquer and sprayed over the offending surface almost like a colour wash. If you are French polishing, a little spirit aniline dye can be mixed with transparent polish; the surface is then polished in the usual way with a rubber (see Chapter 6) until the desired level of correction is achieved.

It is tempting to use a strong colour in the belief that this will have the desired effect quicker. In reality you will replace one problem with another by creating another undesirable hue. Always use a very weak colour in successive, thin applications; colour correction is a *gradual* process. Apply as many coats as are required – the first application may not produce any noticeable effect at all, but the second and subsequent applications should demonstrate a considerable change.

Varnishing presents a more difficult problem, as very few dyes will dissolve in the solvents (unless water-based varnishes have been used, in which case water-based aniline dyes are ideal). The nature of varnishing also means that relatively thick coats are applied, giving rise to the danger of overcolouring. In many cases the answer is to prepare some spirit aniline dye and mix it with a little transparent French polish, applying the resulting mixture with a rubber. Once the colour is satisfactory, continue varnishing normally (see Chapter 7).

THE COLOURING PROCEDURE

In theory, colouring can take place any time after staining. In practice it is better to tackle the problem after the first coat of polish has been applied, as it is only at this point that you will have any real idea of the final colour. By applying an effective sealing coat, any mistakes made in the colour can usually be reversed; for example, by stripping and starting again! Colour applied directly on to a stained but as yet unsealed surface may create problems as the dye sinks into the wood.

It is sometimes helpful to make and follow a pattern. Many items to be coloured can be divided into a number of different parts, or physically disassembled for the purpose of polishing. In such cases, take one of the parts (say, a table top, or drawer front), 'colour it down' to the correct hue and use it as a pattern, or reference colour, to which all the other parts must be matched.

Allow more than adequate time for the previous coat to dry, otherwise you will be in danger of 'lifting' the colour and causing patchiness.

GENERAL DARKENING

A stain is frequently the right colour when applied to the wood but, when you begin to polish, it can become apparent that, while more or less correct, it is not dark enough. In such cases you will need to darken the surface without changing its basic colour, and for this you should use pigments rather than dyes.

PIGMENTS

Pigments have the necessary properties to successfully impart an opacity to the polished finish which effectively darkens it. They do not dissolve in any of the polishes a woodfinisher uses, and so will have an obliterating effect.

For darkening, you will need to make up a 'darkening polish'. Mix a little vegetable black pigment in the polish, making sure it is completely dispersed. Add a little reddish pigment (i.e. burnt sienna) to this mixture, and completely disperse it. This should produce a slightly muddy brown.

Guidance on exact quantities of pigment to use cannot be given, as this depends on individual circumstances. The colour balance of the darkening polish will be determined by the amount of darkening required. Sometimes the balance needs to be towards the red, sometimes towards the black. This may not sound very helpful, but colouring is not an exact science, being very much a subjective art! Experience will improve your skill, and a highly developed colour sense will prove to be invaluable.

It is also difficult to advise specifically on the depth of colour to aim for, as this again depends on the project in question. However, darkening polish should *not* look like paint, so heavily laden with pigment that it is solid in colour. It must be fairly transparent because the end result is achieved by the application of successive thin coats. Too much pigment will cause the polish to dry as a solid, obliterating coat.

Fig 8.4 The effect of a 'darkening' polish.

Darkening polish should be laid on the work in thin coats using a fad (see Chapter 6). Fig 8.4 shows a before and after effect of darkening.

PAINTING OUT BLEMISHES

RING MARKS OR CLOUDY AREAS

Fig 8.5 shows the sort of blemish that should be corrected using the painting-out technique. This ring on a French polished surface was caused by a glass or cup with a wet base. In most cases, white ring marks result from moisture entering the polish film and discolouring it. The technique for repairing these blemishes is described in Chapter 9, but in this case the polish has been taken off the wood altogether and must be repaired with a colouring polish, as shown in Fig 8.6.

The process is as follows:

1 The light area is stained to bring it close to the colour required.
2 Make up a darkening polish. In this case the colour balance was towards black, requiring a little more pigment to be added to the polish, making it more opaque.

Fig 8.5 The colour and the polish of this surface have been completely removed by a wet object.

3 Paint the colour on to the blemish using a very fine artist's brush (perhaps a 00). Use very short strokes so that the colour does not appear as great blotches. The strokes will finally begin to overlap and give the appearance of grain texture, totally masking the blemish.

4 When the polish has dried give the whole surface a few coats of French polish, completing the restoration process. With varnished work, protect the recoloured area by varnishing the whole surface.

CIGARETTE BURNS

Fig 8.7 shows a more difficult case of painting out – a cigarette burn. These are a real challenge. It is very difficult, if not impossible, to mask the blemish in a way that will not be detected. However, the visual impact of the burn can be reduced by painting it out in such a way that the area closely resembles the surrounding surface. Even though it may still be noticeable, it will be a big improvement, as Fig 8.8 shows.

Fig 8.6 The blemish is rectified by staining and painting out.

The process is as follows:

1 The blemish will be masked by overlaying it with different colours. You need to begin by determining which colours to use. Look at the surface and you will see that there is a base colour, usually the lightest. Mix up your 'paint' in French polish or varnish (depending on the medium concerned) so that its colour resembles the base colour – you may need more than one pigment to do this.

2 Use a fine artist's brush to lay this colour down with short strokes, along the grain. This will hide the blemish but will leave a definite 'smudge'. Allow to dry.

3 Next, determine the next lightest colour, make up your paint, and brush it on to the patch. You need to be careful here: the aim is not to cover the whole patch but to begin simulating the grain texture, or figure, using short brush strokes.

4 There may be other colours which need to be overlaid, and

Fig 8.7 Cigarette burns cut deep into the fibres of the wood.

Fig 8.8 Here, pigments have been used to 'paint out' the cigarette burn; however, the depression will often remain as a shadowy blur even after painting out.

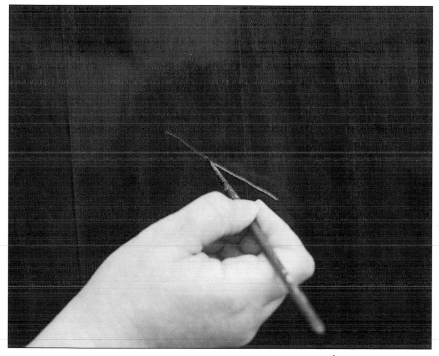

Fig 8.9 Colouring out a scratch.

this is done in ascending order of darkness, beginning with the lightest colour and ending with the darkest. You will rarely need more than three colours. Always allow plenty of drying time between coats.

5 When the process is complete, allow a couple of hours drying time and then seal the colour with a coat of clear polish (French polish or varnish), applied without any pressure, using a rubber. When dry, give the whole surface a coat or two of polish.

DEEP SCRATCHES

These are easier to handle:

1 Mix up your paint with slightly less pigment so that it is not opaque.

2 Colour out the scratch by painting along it with a fine artist's brush (see Fig 8.9); as the paint is less opaque you may need two or three applications.

3 Seal with polish, also applied by brush.

4 Refinish the whole surface to 'blend in' (see Chapter 9).

9
REFINISHING

FURNITURE

Knowing when and how to refinish furniture is often regarded as a problem area. However, care and common sense will go a long way to solving the problems.

PATINA

The importance of patination – the mellowing of a surface through use, generations of hand-polishing and exposure to light – cannot be ignored when dealing with restoration work, as it is an indicator of age and, by implication, of authenticity. Its absence makes collectors suspicious and reduces the value of an item in the sale room. However, a line must be drawn between genuine patina and grime, or real damage.

Patina is a property of the polish film and wood surface – a part of the furniture, not something on the surface that can be removed by cleaning. For example, it is generally accepted that minor dents and scratches are legitimate forms of patination, since they are not really disfiguring. A cigarette burn, on the other hand, is damage, which it is permissible to repair. Stripping old polished surfaces and staining and repolishing, even using traditional methods and materials, will destroy valuable patina and must only be carried out under extreme circumstances. Even then, it must be done by a professional in such a way that will retain or restore as much patina as possible.

In many instances, a good restorer can reproduce the patina if stripping cannot be avoided. This is a highly skilled technique demanding a thorough knowledge of how things should look. After restoration, the piece should ideally appear as if it has never been touched.

The bottom line is: wherever possible, avoid stripping an old surface. There are usually better alternatives, especially if that surface is basically sound.

CRITERIA FOR STRIPPING

Start from the premise that stripping is unnecessary and undesirable unless:

▌ The old finish is badly damaged; i.e. flaking off or badly worn.

■ The new finish is not compatible with the old; i.e. a French polish cannot be put over an ordinary varnish because it will peel off due to lack of adhesion.

■ The old finish is known to be a modern lacquer; i.e. it cannot be repaired because a good bond between old and new finishes will not be obtained. (This does not apply to polyurethane varnishes, which can be repaired successfully if not too far gone.)

■ The colour of the wood has been badly faded by strong sunlight and needs to be restored.

Under no circumstances should an old and possibly valuable piece of furniture be stripped by anyone other than a professional restorer. Other items can be refinished by the amateur without losing value, but even here it is not always necessary to strip; always regard it as a last resort. If you are sure it is the right course, refer to page 118 for detailed information on the processes involved.

IDENTIFYING FINISHES

Before testing to determine the nature of the material, you can more or less infer what the finish is likely to be by the age of the object. Anything over 50 years old is likely to be finished in a spirit-based varnish or French polish. Post-war furniture will very likely be finished in an early nitrocellulose, and contemporary furniture will be finished in one of the catalysed lacquers.

It is difficult to be *absolutely* certain about such things, because an old piece may have been refinished fairly recently, in which case the finish is likely to be a cellulose-based lacquer if refinished professionally, or polyurethane varnish if finished by an amateur. The latter will probably be characterized by brushmarks, possibly with dust specks and small fragments of bristle.

The nature of a finish will be discovered partly by testing, partly by knowledge of an item's age and partly by knowledge of the piece's history. If you don't know what finish has been applied, Table 4 explains how to test with solvents to arrive at an answer.

The table works by a process of elimination, asking questions and guiding you to others. Start at 1, and if the answer is that the finish will not soften with methylated spirit, you are told to move to 2, and so on, until you arrive at a final answer.

When testing a surface with solvents or by scraping, choose a small and inconspicuous area. The solvent should be applied with a soft

TABLE 4

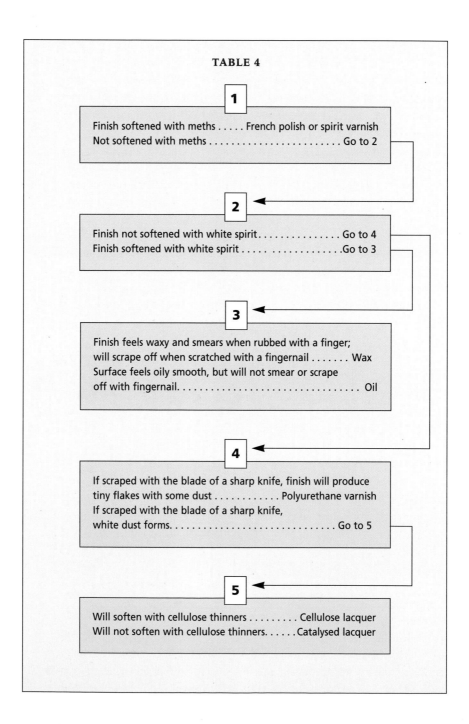

1

Finish softened with meths . . . . . French polish or spirit varnish
Not softened with meths . . . . Go to 2

2

Finish not softened with white spirit. . . . . Go to 4
Finish softened with white spirit . . . . .Go to 3

3

Finish feels waxy and smears when rubbed with a finger;
will scrape off when scratched with a fingernail . . . . Wax
Surface feels oily smooth, but will not smear or scrape
off with fingernail. . . . . Oil

4

If scraped with the blade of a sharp knife, finish will produce
tiny flakes with some dust . . . . Polyurethane varnish
If scraped with the blade of a sharp knife,
white dust forms. . . . . Go to 5

5

Will soften with cellulose thinners . . . . Cellulose lacquer
Will not soften with cellulose thinners. . . . . .Catalysed lacquer

clean cloth, but begin by cleaning the area with soap and water to remove grime that could confuse the result of the test.

These are easily repaired. Marks caused by heat, moisture and handling are removed by wiping over the surface with white spirit or pure turpentine, allowed to dry again and then recoated with wax polish or furniture oil.

FRENCH POLISH

REVIVING

A neglected polished surface will be dull with accumulated dust and old wax. If it has been regularly polished with an aerosol polish or with wax pastes over a long period, the surface can also become very greasy and dull. Such a surface will benefit from the application of a reviver (recipe 1 on page 145 will be sufficient for most tasks, but if the work is very heavily soiled, even after washing, recipe 3 is an alternative). The process is as follows:

1 Clean the surface with a solution of one teaspoon of washing soda in a pint (0.56l) of warm water, using a well wrung-out chamois leather.

2 Allow to dry, and then test for any remaining deposits of wax by rubbing the surface with a fingernail. If it is still dirty, greasy deposits will lift off.

3 Wash again until all the dirt has been removed. After drying there will still be a dullness and possibly some whitish streaks due to residue. Remove these with the reviver.

4 Apply the reviver sparingly with a pad of stockinette, working a small area at a time with circular movements. As the area brightens, change to straight strokes, and finish off by buffing with a clean piece of stockinette. Revive the whole surface in this way.

5 When the whole surface is revived, buff with a clean pad.

REPOLISHING

If after all this the French polish is still dull, or even shows signs of wear, it will need to be repolished to bring back the shine. The process is as follows:

1 It will not be necessary to strip, but the old polish should be prepared first by cutting back with 600 grit wet-or-dry paper, used wet (a little detergent in the water acts as a wetting agent and makes the task easier). The aim is

to create a uniform dullness over the whole surface, thus keying it in preparation for refinishing.

2 Once the surface has been cut back in this way, refinish with French polish thinned a little by methylated spirit (one part methylated spirit to three parts polish).

3 Finish by stiffing (see Chapter 6, page 76).

Of course, all this assumes that the French polish is without serious blemishes. There may be marks similar or identical to those discussed in Chapter 8 which require special treatment.

RING MARKS OR CLOUDY AREAS

White marks (caused by water or heat as previously explained) can easily be removed from French polished surfaces, or at least, reduced. The process is as follows:

1 Mix some cigarette ash with raw linseed oil into a paste.

2 Apply the paste to the mark with a finger wrapped in a cloth. Use a fair amount of pressure, rubbing along the grain over the ring (see Fig 9.1). Faint areas will respond quite quickly, while heavier marks may need two or more

applications over a period of a few days.

3 Wipe off any surplus oil, and clean the entire surface with a reviver. The marks may not disappear altogether but will look a lot less obvious.

DARK RING MARKS

Dark rings occur if very hot dishes are allowed to rest on the surface; the heat discolours the wood beneath. Such scorch marks must be treated in the same way as cigarette burns.

Dark marks are also caused by water penetrating the polish and discolouring the wood (see Fig 9.2). The only cure is to strip the old polish and bleach out the stain with oxalic acid or 20 vol. hydrogen peroxide. (See Chapter 4 for information on mixing and using these bleaches, but remember that both oxalic acid and hydrogen peroxide are dangerous substances and must be used in accordance with the health and safety information on the packaging.) The surface can then be restained and repolished as required. This is drastic action, and should always be given careful consideration before proceeding. If you can live with the marks, do so rather than risk ruining a good piece of furniture.

REMOVING RING MARKS

Fig 9.1(a) Before. A fair amount of pressure applied with a finger along the grain will be required to remove these white ring marks and cloudy areas, caused by water.

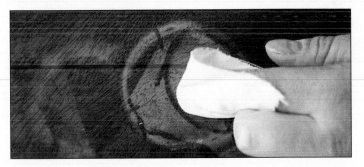

Fig 9.1(b) Applying the paste.

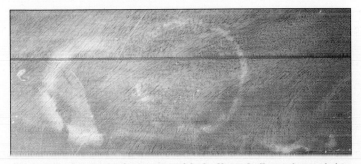

Fig 9.1(c) After. Several attempts with the linseed oil may be needed to remove the ring completely.

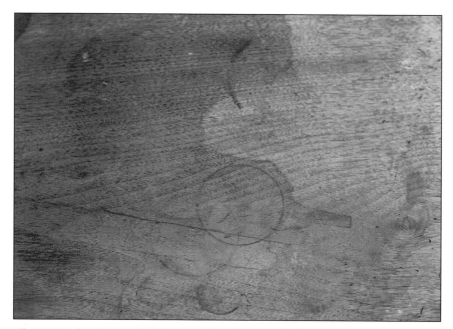

Fig 9.2 Dark water marks. This surface has been very badly abused: the rings were caused by wet vases which were left long enough for the water to penetrate the wood, and the larger patch is probably the result of an overflow from a plant holder that has gone unnoticed. As a general rule, the shape and intensity of a dark patch is a good indicator of the cause.

INK RINGS

Desks and bureaux are often found with small black, red or blue rings caused by ink. There is very little that can be done to remove these. Under no circumstances attempt to strip a valuable piece. You can try bleaching the ring with a little weak oxalic acid, but do not leave it on the area for too long or it will produce its own mark. If the acid is going to work, it will do so quickly. Clean it off afterwards with warm water and detergent, and buff dry.

In those cases where a ring mark shows up as an area of polish which has been removed completely, you will need to paint out the blemish (see Chapter 8, page 105).

SCRATCHES

Very minor scratches can be darkened by rubbing over with a little raw linseed oil and wiping off the surplus. If the scratch is very white, due to the wood beneath also being scratched, mix in a little powder pigment of an appropriate colour. Major scratches may necessitate stripping and repolishing. See Chapter 8 for guidance on colouring out scratches.

FLAKING OR
CRAZED POLISH

There is little to do here other than strip and repolish, as the old finish is in the process of disintegration (see Fig 9.3).

BURNS

These have to be either ignored, painted out (see Chapter 8), or given professional repair.

POLYURETHANE
VARNISH AND
SYNTHETIC LACQUERS

Repairs to such surfaces are generally limited. You may be able to treat white heat and water marks, or disguise minor scratches as described above, but the only sure method is to strip and repolish.

Polyurethane can be rubbed down with fine wet-or-dry abrasive to try to remove a blemish, and then given a new coat of varnish. In any event, if you intend to recoat polyurethane you must provide a key for the new coat in this way.

Fig 9.3 This polish is flaking off the surface and beyond refinishing. It will have to be stripped and replaced.

JOINERY

POLYURETHANE AND YACHT VARNISHES

If the varnish film is mostly sound, with perhaps a little flaking and some bare patches, the following procedure should be adopted:

1 Wash down the surface, avoiding bare areas and allow it to dry.
2 Rub down with 240 grit abrasive.
3 Wipe over the surface with a tack rag.
4 Recoat with one or two coats of varnish with the wet-or-dry treatment between them.

If varnish stains have been used and the surface has bare areas (even small ones), you may need to strip and treat as a new surface for revarnishing. Otherwise the bare areas may show up darker than the rest after refinishing.

Peeling varnish is an indication of progressive loss of adhesion, and it is wise to strip and revarnish.

MICROPOROUS VARNISHES

These are treated in exactly the same way as polyurethane, except that only one coat of new varnish is applied. Always remember that a microporous varnish cannot be used over a non-MVP because its permeability will be lost. Any other type of varnish must be stripped off first.

PRESERVATIVES

These tend to weather and fade (if coloured) naturally, and, provided they are not a varnish-based compound, they can simply be recoated. If you intend to use a new water-based compound over a solvent-based original coat such as creosote, make sure the old material is well weathered. Treat at a minimum every two years to ensure maximum protection. See Chapter 10 for more information on preservatives.

STRIPPING

Instructions for the use of proprietary paint and varnish strippers are given on the side of the cans. However, you should bear in mind the following to obtain good results.

PREPARING FOR STRIPPING

Proprietary strippers are based on a powerful solvent, called methylene chloride, and alcohol. This means they evaporate, and the fumes can be very dangerous in confined spaces. Good ventilation is essential, and if you have chronic respiratory problems or are sensitive to fumes, use a respirator. Always be sure to wear protective clothing including heavy-duty rubber gloves of industrial quality – household gloves will dissolve!

Put down lots of newspaper on the floor beneath the work and around it, and add plenty around the work to allow for splashes (see Fig 9.4). Have an old bucket filled with water to hand, so that as the softened varnish is lifted off the wood it can be dropped into the bucket out of harm's way.

As shown in Fig 9.4, dismantle the piece as far as it is possible to do so and remove any drawer furniture such as handles and hinges to reduce obstructions. This 'breaking down' of a piece allows the work to be sectioned off into manageable stages.

Do not use shavehook scrapers when removing softened polish, as they tend to dig into the wood. Instead, modify an old cabinet scraper or wallpaper scraper as shown in Fig 9.5. Use 00 grade wire wool to remove material from awkward places such as carvings and mouldings – do not use a scraper here, as it will dig in and damage the wood.

Different brands of stripper are very similar, but do look for the magic phrases 'non-caustic' or 'non-acid', meaning they will be kind to the wood.

HINTS ON STRIPPING

The first coat of stripper should be brushed on like paint, providing a key by roughening the surface. After a couple of minutes, apply a very generous second coat, and leave this for at least 10 minutes on

Fig 9.4 Preparations for stripping: use plenty of newspapers to protect the floor and dismantle the piece as far as possible.

MODIFIED TOOLS FOR STRIPPING

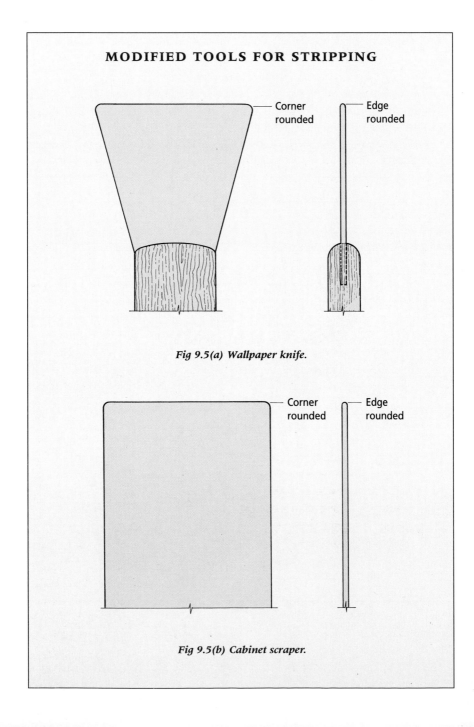

Corner rounded

Edge rounded

Fig 9.5(a) Wallpaper knife.

Corner rounded

Edge rounded

Fig 9.5(b) Cabinet scraper.

varnished surfaces. Use it liberally; whilst expensive stuff, skimping will only result in having to spend more time on the job and using more stripper. There should be a substantial amount of stripper on the surface but not so much that it runs all over the place. Work it well into crevices and corners with a stabbing action of the brush.

Always neutralize stripped surfaces afterwards, even if the stripper is described as self-neutralizing. I always use methylated spirit or white spirit (even with strippers that describe themselves as suitable for neutralization with water), for two reasons: first, there is no grain raising, so the wood doesn't go 'fuzzy', and second, because the work dries much faster, allowing me to strip and stain in a single day. Neutralizing with water results in a long drying period, especially in cold weather. Never try to refinish if the work has not dried out properly.

Sometimes a finish will resist the action of strippers, even to the point where they have no effect whatsoever. This occurs with some of the catalysed lacquers, and there is very little you can do about it. Stripping with abrasives is one possibility, but this is laborious and only feasible on flat surfaces, so you may have to resort to commercial stripping companies.

DIPPING TANKS

I am often asked about commercial stripping and the effect of dipping tanks. There are terrible – and often true – horror stories about furniture falling apart and wood darkening or splitting, but it is not fair to generalize.

Under no circumstances send mahogany, walnut or oak furniture to be dipped if the tanks use a caustic solution, as this may cause bad discoloration. In addition, prolonged immersion in these caustic solutions frequently results in efflorescence later as the wood dries out at home. Prolonged immersion may cause the caustic soda to become deeply absorbed into the wood. Efflorescence is the appearance of a white powdery deposit on the surface, indicating inadequate neutralization of the caustic, and it may reappear even if cleaned off. If this occurs, wipe over the wood with a generous helping of white malt vinegar in warm water. Allow to dry but leave for a few weeks before risking any refinishing.

There are a number of stripping firms who specialize in non-caustic dipping. The stripper is solvent-based and much safer for your furniture and joinery. I have found the results of non-caustic dipping very satisfactory. Water is still used at the end of the process to neutralize residue, but there is no extended immersion, no discoloration, and joints which were sound on entering the tank remain so. Problems can be experienced with veneered work however, as even small cracks or bubbles can result in lifting.

TREATMENT
AFTER STRIPPING

After stripping, the wood is treated as if it were a new surface, and can be smoothed with abrasives, stained and repolished. You may experience a little fuzziness on the surface if water has been used to neutralize the stripper, but in general, because the surface has already been smoothed when originally polished,

very little preparation is needed. Use only a fine abrasive (240 or 320 grit).

Veneers present a tricky problem in that they are very thin, and extra care needs to be exercised. Use a 320 grit abrasive and work cautiously to remove any raised fibres, not the veneer itself.

If you find that a stain will not take properly, this is likely to be due to incomplete stripping. The stain simply lies on top of the wood, so that when wiped over it is merely taken off again, or causes patchiness where it is absorbed in some areas but not in others (see Fig 9.6). The only solution to this problem is to use the stripper again, and to rub over the work with 000 steel wool after about 10 minutes. The stripper is again neutralized as already described.

Fig 9.6 The light area shows where a stain has not taken, due to the surface not being completely stripped.

10

PROTECTING TIMBER

Timber has phenomenal durability when environmental conditions are right, but in adverse conditions wooden structures can be destroyed in a frighteningly short time.

It is an unpleasant fact of life that any naturally occurring organic material will have at least one living organism capable of using it as a food supply. Wood is no exception to this rule, which has evolved to ensure that nutrients locked up inside organic material become recycled. The main agents in this process are insects, usually at the larval stage, and fungi. The two are frequently linked, in that the tunnels created by the burrowing larvae allow the entry of fungal spores. This invasion by fungi is often an independent subsequent event, but sometimes the insects themselves carry the fungal spores into the wood as the larvae burrow through.

A less obvious risk to wood is strong sunlight. Long-term exposure to UV radiation results in chemical changes in the structure of wood fibres, bringing about a degrading of the wood.

In nature, insect infestation of wood (either living or dead) is usually the first stage in the recycling process. There are many species that spend part of their life cycle in wood, but as far as furniture and structural timbers are concerned we are worried by a smaller number, mostly those that can live in relatively dry conditions. However, fungal attack causes the moisture level of wood to increase, and in these conditions the wood can undergo secondary insect infestation, by weevils or woodlice, for example. These insects are unwelcome, of course, but in these circumstances must be considered harmless as the only reason for their presence is the already irretrievably decayed state of the wood – they are not able to survive in healthy wood. Under this onslaught wood can be reduced to a pile of powder, with only strands of the harder areas remaining intact.

The most obvious signs of insect infestation are the exit holes – the points where the adult insects have chewed their way out before flying off. The adult stage is normally short-lived, and, after mating, the female lays her eggs on the surface of the timber. After they have hatched, the larvae burrow their way into the wood and the cycle begins again (see Fig 10.1). The larval stage can last for several years, depending on the species, during which time they chew their way through the structure, forming tunnels. The exit holes ('worm holes' or 'flight holes') are the points where the adult beetle has escaped from the wood, and are not a reliable indicator of the true extent of the internal damage caused by the larvae eating their way through the wood. However, a large area covered with holes should be taken as an indication of very serious infestation.

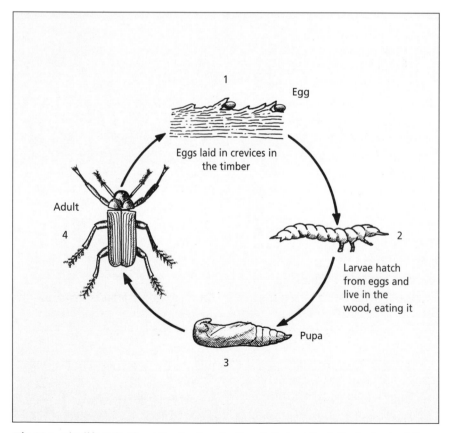

Fig 10.1 The life cycle of woodboring insects: the adult stage is relatively short, while the highly destructive larval stage may last for years.

COMMON FURNITURE BEETLE

Otherwise known as woodworm, this is one of the commonest of timber pests, and is or has been present in most old houses and a good deal of old furniture. The adult beetle emerges during the summer months, an event often marked by the appearance of fine wood dust (frass). The beetles only live for a couple of weeks, and mate soon after emerging (see Fig 10.2(a)).

The female lays her eggs in crevices, on end grain, or on rough timber, never on smooth surfaces. When buying old furniture, it pays to inspect the backs, the inside of frames, and other hidden areas, as these will be favoured by the beetle. The larval stage lasts for at least two years, depending on the temperature, humidity and type of timber. The ideal conditions for beetles are a temperature of around 22°C and an air humidity of around 50%. Therefore, they favour old houses without central heating.

The exit holes of the furniture beetle are about 1/16in (1.5mm–2mm) in diameter (see Fig 10.2(b)). Recent holes are light in colour on the inside, while older ones tend to darken with age and accumulated dirt. Frass is also associated with these. You may also see a number of very small holes (less than 1mm) situated nearby. These are caused by small insects called chalcids, that prey on the furniture beetle larvae. Their larvae live as parasites on the beetle larvae, killing them in the process. The adult chalcid either emerges through an old beetle exit hole or creates very small ones of its own.

DEATHWATCH BEETLE

This is one of the larger woodboring beetles, whose presence is almost exclusively confined to structural timbers made of oak. The eggs are laid in April or May, and the larvae may take 5–10 years to complete their stage of the life cycle before emerging as adults. The exit holes are large, at between 1/8in and almost 1/4in (3–5mm) in diameter (see Figs 10.3(a) and 10.3(b)).

LONG-HORN BEETLE

This species also attacks structural timbers, though not exclusively oak (see Fig 10.4(a)) and can cause extensive damage. Some species attack softwood, while other prefer hardwood. The larvae of the former are frequently imported into the house in bark-covered timber. The exit holes are a characteristic oval shape (see Fig 10.4(b)).

COMMON FURNITURE BEETLE (WOODWORM)

Photograph courtesy of Rentokil Ltd.

Fig 10.2(a) Common furniture beetle.

Photograph courtesy of Rentokil Ltd.

Fig 10.2(b) Exit holes of the common furniture beetle. Note also the small exit holes made by the chalcid beetle.

DEATHWATCH BEETLE

Photograph courtesy of Rentokil Ltd.

Fig 10.3(a) Deathwatch beetle.

Photograph courtesy of Rentokil Ltd.

Fig 10.3(b) Deathwatch beetle flight holes.

LONG-HORN BEETLE

Photograph courtesy of Rentokil Ltd.

Fig 10.4(a) Long-horn beetle.

Photograph courtesy of Rentokil Ltd.

Fig 10.4(b) Long-horn beetle flight holes.

PREVENTION

As the whole process of attack by insects is a natural one, it is frequently possible to transfer the creatures when bringing timber indoors. Any felled timber which has spent some time lying around, especially if it has seen spring and summer in that state, should be treated with suspicion. It pays to remove the bark and sapwood before bringing such timber into the house.

Other preventive measures include the maintenance of a dry environment. Centrally heated houses are, paradoxically, a fairly hostile environment, as while the temperature may be ideal there is usually a reduction in air humidity, causing wood moisture levels to reduce also.

DETECTION
AND ERADICATION

While prevention is always better than cure it is not always successful, so you need to rely on eradication. The brief descriptions of life cycles above indicate that the spring and summer months are crucial to the insects (when they mate and lay their eggs), and these are the months when you should be vigilant in looking out for tell-tale signs. Examine all the surfaces of the wood, especially the normally unseen areas, for new holes. If you find an area where the holes seem particularly light in colour or there is frass around, assume an attack.

Large-scale attacks to structural timbers by furniture beetles, or attacks by deathwatch or house long-horned beetles should be dealt with by one of the pest control organizations. The chemicals required to eradicate these pests are poisonous and their use in a large-scale operation must be professionally supervised.

Small-scale attacks, such as those associated with furniture, are quite easy to deal with yourself. The aim of pest control is to prevent reinfestation and destroy any larvae still present in the wood. Although the fact that the holes appear when the larvae are on their way out may make you feel you are closing the door after the horse has bolted, bear in mind that there may be larvae still in the wood at a different stage of their life cycle. Treatment of the infected wood and of pieces situated nearby will hopefully kill the remaining pests and prevent future cross-infestation.

TREATMENT

There is little to choose between the various proprietary woodworm treatment fluids, as they are all strong, efficient insecticides.

With furniture, the vulnerable areas to be treated, as already indicated, are those not normally visible: the backs, the inside of the tops of legs, and the tops and bottoms of carcasses – the framework of the furniture. Show wood is rarely the source of the problem, but it may exhibit the effects with unsightly exit holes. Unpolished wood should be treated by brushing the fluid on and letting it soak in, with exit holes injected, as described below. *Do not* do this over polished show wood because:

▌ Eggs are not normally laid in these areas, making it a waste of effort.
▌ The poisonous residue left on the surface becomes a danger to children and pets.
▌ The residue dulls the polished surface.

The best way to treat woodworm is to inject the fluid into the exit, or flight, holes; many woodworm treatment fluid containers come with a spout to make this even easier (see Fig 10.5). This achieves greater penetration of the wood and also makes it more difficult for any remaining larvae to spread or for new larvae to enter via the old holes. It is not necessary to inject every hole, as they frequently interconnect. Inject one hole every square inch, but be careful – you will discover how they join up when the fluid squirts out of other holes!

Always remember these fluids are toxic, and be sure to wash your hands after use. Try to limit contact with the skin as much as possible, and do not attempt to spray the liquid. The odour left by fluid treatment will disappear after about a day.

In addition to woodworm fluids, there are also special anti-woodworm wax polishes containing the insecticide. This is ideal for treatment of suitable show wood where flight holes are evident.

After treatment, keep a regular eye on treated pieces for a couple of years to ensure full elimination has taken place. As a further precaution, paint the unseen areas of the wood again during the spring following the initial treatment.

FUNGAL ATTACK

While fungi are, in biological terms, among the most important living organisms on the planet, as they are responsible for decomposing organic matter, thereby releasing materials for recycling, they are not particularly welcome when their action causes timber to disintegrate before our eyes. The problem may be compounded by the fact that the

Fig 10.5 Injecting flight holes with woodworm fluid, using an inexpensive applicator which can be bought separately. Smaller tins have an injector incorporated into the top.

softening effect on the wood fibres encourages animal pests, such as woodlice, to invade.

Fungi propagate by spores which are dispersed into the air, which can lie dormant for long periods before springing to life again if conditions for fungal growth are right. The most important of these conditions is moisture.

WET ROT

Most timber attacking fungi prefer a moisture level of around 30–50%. The vulnerable timbers are all exterior constructions, timbers in contact with the soil or any outside ground, and any timbers in an environment giving rise to high moisture levels, inside or out.

Inside, poor ventilation can cause this, or perhaps a flood. Providing recently soaked wood is dried out quickly there is little danger of serious fungal damage. However, repeated or extended periods of high moisture levels will eventually lead to wet rot unless adequate protection is afforded.

The first sign of fungal attack often takes the form of patches of blue-black discoloration, caused by mildew-type fungi. These attacks are not particularly damaging, but should be taken as a sign that if left unchecked, the wood will deteriorate as fungi take over.

The damage is caused by the way fungi feed. This is a process called external digestion, whereby filament-like fibres of the fungus produce digestive juices that are sent into the wood. The wood fibres are literally digested outside the fungus, and the nutrients are then absorbed into the fungus. The wood becomes soft and spongy, and its moisture level rises, making the conditions for further deterioration ideal. The process is almost self-perpetuating. In the end, the structure of the timber is destroyed, and it crumbles away as a soggy, fibrous mass. This process is known as wet rot, and Fig 10.6 shows the kind of damage it can cause.

Fig 10.6 If wet rot is not dealt with in the early stages, large-scale destruction is inevitable. The disintegrated, fibrous mass which the timber becomes will lead to secondary infestation by invertebrates such as woodlice.

In extreme cases it will be necessary to cut away the affected timber and replace with new, sound wood. That said, the progress of wet rot is relatively slow compared with the rampant spread of dry rot.

DRY ROT

The fungus that causes dry rot, *Merulius lacrymans*, will thrive in timber with a moisture level as low as 20%. Once the fungus has established itself, it can spread to dry timbers (hence the name), because it is able to survive on the moisture gained from the original damp timber. The fungus can spread very rapidly in two ways: first, it will generate millions of spores that become distributed through the air; second, it is able to send out from the main body many fibres, called hyphae, which seek out new timber, and may even pass over several metres of masonry and cement in their search, even though these provide no nourishment whatsoever. The main body of the fungus will supply these hyphae with nourishment until new timber has been located. As a result, dry rot can spread with frightening speed (see Figs 10.7 and 10.8).

Dry rot is best dealt with by a professional builder or company that specializes in pest eradication. The treatment usually involves a radical removal of timber adjacent to the attack, because you can never be too sure how far the hyphae have reached. A liberal application of fungicides on remaining and replacement timber then ensures that eradication is complete.

PREVENTION

As fungi generally attack damp timber, the best preventive measure is to ensure that timbers remain dry, either by eliminating sources of moisture, or ensuring that vulnerable timbers have adequate ventilation. Timber thus treated will rarely be attacked, but regular inspection is advisable. Furniture is unlikely to be attacked by fungi, as the moisture level in the timber in even the worst domestic environments is unlikely to reach a vulnerable level.

Timbers which are likely to be constantly wet and exposed to moisture will need preventive treatment, usually in the form of an annual or biennial application of preservative, depending on the amount of exposure and weathering.

PRESERVATIVES

All wood preservatives are poisons; their intention is to kill off wood-attacking insects and fungi. Many of

Photograph courtesy of Rentokil Ltd.

Fig 10.7 The characteristic appearance of dry rot.

the newer formulations make the claim of being harmless to plants and pets, and this is certainly true once the stuff has dried, but during use they remain very unpleasant substances.

Manufacturers tend to formulate their products for specific purposes, and there is a bewildering array of products to choose from. Ask yourself the following questions to help you make a decision as to which preservative to choose:

▌ Is it for internal or external use?

▌ Will I be painting the wood or finishing it in some other way after the preservative has been applied?

▌ What decorative properties do I require? Am I applying the preservative to a garden fence made of rough timber, or to a new front door which must have a high quality, attractive and resilient finish?

Photograph courtesy of Rentokil Ltd.

Fig 10.8 Dry rot damage.

CONSTRUCTIONAL TIMBERS

The oldest and cheapest preservative is creosote. This is a coal tar product which, while effective, is toxic to plants, wildlife and pets while wet, not to mention unpleasant to work with and smelly!

Modern preparations are based on synthetic chemicals, and there is a general tendency towards meeting the market demand for 'safe' products, which are non-toxic once dry. While most of these preparations are solvent-based, some are water-based, and these have a number of attractions, not least the lack of odour. However, water-based preservatives are only suitable for rough-sawn timber such as fencing, and are often marketed as suitable for garden timbers.

Timbers in contact with the ground or exposed to extreme weather need the deeply penetrating preservatives designed for these conditions. These are usually formulated to give extra protection against fungal decay, the risk of which is increased for timbers which are likely to be wet for extended periods.

Almost all of these products are strongly pigmented to provide additional protection against UV, which is damaging to the wood and the preservative. UV is an effective decomposer of organic material – the high-energy rays actually break down chemical bonds – so special UV-absorbing pigments are present in the preservative to reduce this effect.

Colourless preservatives are also available, but should not be used on their own for exterior timbers because of the UV problem. They are suitable for use on internal timbers, and there are many situations where it is desirable to use a preservative without changing the colour of the wood. For example, you may wish to protect wooden floors but retain the natural colour, or paint or varnish vulnerable timbers such as exterior doors or window frames, in which case the colourless preservative can be applied as an initial coat and not affect the final finish. Wooden structures with a green tinge, often found in horticultural or agricultural settings have been treated with a preservative formulated with a green colour, often used in circumstances where the natural green is a pleasant alternative to darker varieties of pigment. It is a general purpose preservative, and the colour makes it possible to identify treated areas.

SHOW WOOD

A preservative is of little value if it does not penetrate the surface of the wood, and the deeper the penetration the greater the protection. It is also a great advantage if, after application of a preservative, the surface resists water penetration. Many of the preservatives of the type described above do offer some protection against water, thanks to the waxes and oils used in their formulation, but they may not provide the decorative properties of varnish. In the past, yacht varnish (see Chapter 7) would have been used to decorate exterior timbers, but, although it provides some protection from UV radiation and has great flexibility, it has limited durability if the wood contains moisture.

'Woodstain' is a range of decorative products designed to provide the properties of a physical barrier, protection from UV, and some limited protection from fungal attack. They are pigmented, moisture-permeable varnishes, and the latest generation of these are water-based (acrylic), which are more convenient to use (see Chapter 7).

However, since protection can only be provided to that portion of the wood containing the preservative, woodstains are probably not as effective as preservatives, except against surface mildew and algae. This is especially true if the varnish coat becomes damaged, allowing moisture and fungal spores to penetrate. Therefore, provide the best protection by treating the wood with a colourless preservative prior to using a woodstain varnish. Major joinery manufacturers frequently apply preservatives to their exterior products in the factory.

Fig 10.9 shows a door treated with a modern 'woodstain' product.

Fig 10.9 An exterior door treated with a 'woodstain' product. Note the cloudy appearance of the timber, caused by the opacity of the pigments in the varnish.

No more than two or three coats should usually be applied, or they will become less permeable to internal moisture. Properly applied, such varnishes will last for up to six years with conscientious maintenance (see Chapter 7). One negative feature of these products is that the pigments used in them frequently lead to a slight opacity, especially with the darker tones. As a result the natural figuring of the wood is sometimes partially obliterated.

DRAWBACKS

Slapping on a coat or two of preservative does not automatically provide 100% protection. The chemical will only penetrate a few millimetres into the timber, so the internal structure remains vulnerable. It is possible to increase the level of protection by applying preservative under pressure, but this can only be done under factory conditions. End grain is particularly vulnerable, and such areas need to be well soaked. If time and facilities permit, the ends of posts that will be embedded in the ground should be left soaking in preservative overnight, allowing the natural capillary action to draw the liquid right up into the wood (see Fig 10.10). While expensive, posts with metal bases are a worthwhile investment, preventing the need for premature replacement due to the rotting of the post base.

Remember, anything which damages the surface and creates a break in the protective layer will, in time, lead to the timber being attacked from within. Therefore, any pre-treated timber which is cut must have the freshly exposed surfaces treated.

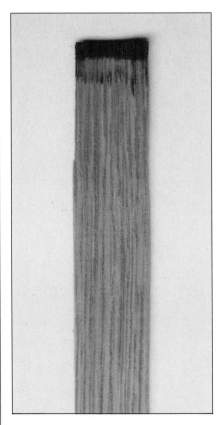

Fig 10.10 The capillary action of end grain, a feature which can be used to your advantage when treating vulnerable timbers with preservatives.

The nature of woodfinishing has changed beyond all recognition over the past four decades or so. No longer are we dealing simply with beeswax and turpentine, linseed oil, alcohol and shellac. There are now some potentially highly dangerous products, produced in answer to the call for cost-efficient coatings with improved mechanical properties (i.e. abilities to resist adverse environmental conditions such as physical knocks, exposure to adverse weather conditions, highly humid environments and exposure to hot sunshine).

Protection begins with knowledge of the hazards associated with the product being used, and manufacturers are obliged to indicate the nature of these hazards on the container.

CLASSIFICATION, PACKAGING AND LABELLING OF DANGEROUS SUBSTANCES REGULATIONS 1984

Fig 11.1 shows an example of a container label providing information aimed at warning the user of the hazards associated with the product. This is now a legal requirement on all containers of hazardous materials sold to the public. The format of such information as laid down by the CPL regulations is as follows:

PRODUCT IDENTIFICATION AND REFERENCE NUMBER

These are specific to the company supplying the product and are a quick and obvious means of identification.

HAZARDOUS SUBSTANCES

The label must name the substances that pose a hazard.

SUBSTANCE IDENTIFICATION NUMBER (UN NUMBER)

This is a number unique to the hazardous substance and acts as another means of identifying the substance.

HAZARD SYMBOLS

Six basic symbols are used to indicate the general nature of the hazard. They are a means of immediate recognition for handlers assisting them and others in adopting appropriate procedures in the event of an emergency.

RISK AND SAFETY PHRASES

These are used to indicate the risks to health that exposure to the substance

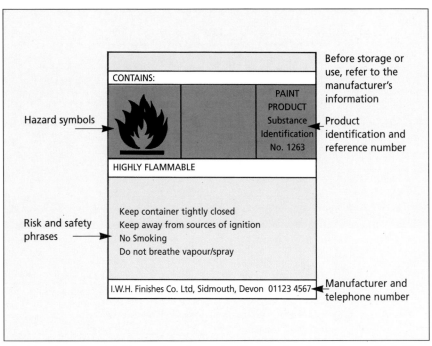

Fig 11.1 Container labelling conforming to the Classification, Packaging and Labelling of Dangerous Substances Regulations 1984.

presents (risk phrases), and to advise how to avoid these risks (safety phrases). Up to four risk phrases may be used – any more would reduce the impact of the information.

MANUFACTURER/SUPPLIER
Should the need arise, this information is present so that the company can be easily contacted and if appropriate, held accountable.

HAZARD SYMBOLS

Fig 11.2 shows the internationally recognized hazard symbols that must by law be used on packaging containing a hazardous substance.

TOXIC
Where serious, acute and chronic health risks, and possibly death, may be involved.

HARMFUL
Where limited health risks may be involved.

CORROSIVE
Where contact with living tissues may destroy them.

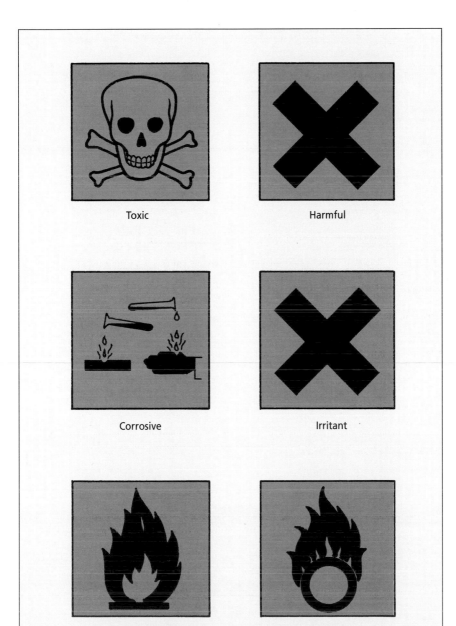

Fig 11.2 The internationally recognized hazard symbols.

IRRITANT

Where inflammation may be caused following contact with the skin or mucous membranes.

HIGHLY FLAMMABLE

Where the product has a flash point below 21°C.

OXIDIZING

Where oxygen is released during a chemical reaction.

These symbols can be used in combination with each other where more than one hazard is involved. Manufacturers have to provide comprehensive Health and Safety Data notes for each hazardous product they supply. Apart from a comprehensive description of the hazardous nature of the product, the notes will include such things as what precautions should be taken during use, what first aid should be administered if a user is subject to exposure, fire prevention and how to safely dispose of the product if it is no longer required or is past its usable lifespan. Always ask for the notes when buying such products, and they will be supplied free.

PROTECTION

Some finishing materials are unpleasant to handle for a variety of reasons, linked to the hazards described above. Perhaps the greatest danger lies in the inhalation of dust and vapours. The risks are not easy to quantify, so it is best to assume that *all* dust generated by sanding (especially machine sanding) and *all* fumes from wood-finishing materials carry a risk.

Good ventilation is always a good idea where volatile materials and large amounts of dust are likely to result from your work. Even with ventilation, it is often wise, as indicated at various points throughout this book, to wear a protective mask or respirator. A respirator, when fitted with the appropriate filter cartridge, will give protection against a wide range of fumes and workshop dust, but always make sure such equipment conforms to the relevant British Standard specification (BS2091). You should also consider the use of a noise attenuator (see Chapter 2) when using noisy machines, particularly if you are operating them for extended periods.

Some of the liquids involved in a number of the techniques described in this book are particularly nasty (e.g. ammonia, hydrogen peroxide and caustic soda) and it is essential to protect yourself against accidental spills and splashes with eye protectors (BS2092), gloves and protective overalls.

12
RECIPES
FOR FINISHES

If you have the time and inclination, many materials and products can be made at home. Should only small quantities be required, it is often more cost-effective to make up these mixtures yourself.

WAX BEAUMONTAGE

FOR COVERING
MINOR SCRATCHES

Melt equal quantities of beeswax and rosin together in a double boiler, starting with the rosin by adding a small amount of turpentine (rosin takes a long time to melt). Once melted add the beeswax. To colour the beaumontage, use pure pigments or artist's oil colours. Liquefy the colour with a little turpentine and pour into the beaumontage mixture, adding enough to make the mixture opaque. Mix, pour the liquid into foil cake cases and allow to cool.

Rub the mixture over minor scratches, allow the deposited wax to harden for a few minutes, and buff.

WAX POLISHES

1) FOR GENERAL PURPOSE USE

- 100g white or yellow beeswax
- 100ml pure turpentine or good quality white spirit

Melt the wax in a double boiler and carefully add the turpentine or white spirit when the wax has melted. Continue to heat, as the wax will have hardened again. When the mixture has clarified, pour into a non-plastic container and allow to set. The polish should be fairly soft (like butter in summer), but it may be necessary to reheat it and add a little more turpentine or white spirit to soften it, or add beeswax to stiffen it up.

2) FOR A HARDER FINISH

- 90g beeswax
- 10g carnauba wax
- 100ml turpentine

Made up in the same way as the first wax polish recipe, this polish will be slightly stiffer and yield a harder finish.

Both of these polishes can be pigmented to create an antiquing wax by stirring a little raw and burnt umber into the molten waxes. The resulting polish will be a grey/brown colour once it has set. When rubbed into the wood it imparts a colour cast like very old wood. The wax also collects in crevices and corners simulating the dirty, dusty effect associated with years of accumulation.

3) FOR USE ON POLISHED SURFACES: BEESWAX FURNITURE CREAM

- 100g beeswax
- 100ml turpentine or white spirit
- 125ml water
- 0.880 ammonia

Melt the wax as before and dissolve it in the turpentine or white spirit. Heat the water but do not bring it to the boil. When the water is hot, quickly pour in the wax/turps solution and stir to emulsify. Add a couple of dashes of ammonia and continue stirring. The ammonia emulsifies the wax and forms a creamy mixture. Continue stirring until cool to prevent separating. A food mixer operating at low speed will take the drudgery out of this procedure.

When the polish cools it becomes quite creamy in consistency, and should be placed in glass jars. Wax creams are not designed to be used on bare wood but as a dressing over a polished surface such as French polish. The water and ammonia clean the surface as the polish is applied. As with all wax polishes, use sparingly.

OIL POLISHES

1) FOR GENERAL POLISHING

- 8 parts raw linseed oil
- 1 part pure turpentine or good quality white spirit
- 1 teaspoon terebene for each $\frac{1}{2}$ pint (0.28l) of mixture (this is optional but does speed up drying)

2) FOR ITEMS USED WITH FOOD

Use food grade oils such as corn, sunflower, safflower, poppy seed and rapeseed for any items used with food, such as salad bowls.

FRENCH POLISH

- 250g shellac flakes
- 500ml methylated spirits

Put the two ingredients into a glass or plastic bottle, agitate to mix and keep in a warm place for at least 24 hours (longer if possible), shaking occasionally. Strain through a pair of tights and rebottle. The mixture is then ready for use.

POLISH REVIVERS

1) FOR GENERAL REVIVING

- 1 part raw linseed oil
- 1 part white malt vinegar
- 1 part methylated spirits

After mixing, the oil will separate out. Shake well to emulsify before and during use, as the ingredients quickly separate. Apply sparingly and rub in a circular motion, finally buffing with a clean soft cloth along the direction of the grain.

2) FOR POLISHED FLOORS

- Equal quantities of paraffin and white malt vinegar

Shake well to emulsify before use and apply sparingly. Buff with a soft cloth to polish.

3) FOR HEAVILY SOILED SURFACES

- 25g (0.9oz) beeswax
- 25g (0.9oz) paraffin wax
- 50g (1.8oz) soap
- 500ml (1.75oz) white spirit or pure turpentine
- 500ml (1.75oz) water

Clean such surfaces first with a teaspoon of washing soda in 500ml of warm water.

Dissolve the soap in hot water. Melt the waxes in a double boiler over a low heat. Remove from the heat and carefully pour in the white spirit or turpentine. The wax will set immediately, so return the mixture to a low heat to melt it again. Reheat the soap solution and pour it into a container large enough to hold both liquids. Stir the soap continuously as you pour in the wax solution to form an emulsion. Continue to stir as the mixture cools to prevent separation. Once cool, pour the creamy liquid into a glass container (plastic will be softened by the turpentine or white spirit).

The reviver will be ready for use after 24 hours when it has set to a gel, and is highly effective. Apply as normal: sparingly with a soft cloth before buffing with a clean cloth.

GLOSSARY

BEAUMONTAGE
A wax 'stopping' used to fill small cracks and holes.

CUT BACK
Another term for sanding down.

DENIB
Removal of nibs (specks of dust) from varnished or painted surfaces, using a fine-grade abrasive.

FRASS
Dust created by the boring of furniture beetles.

HAREWOOD
Sycamore wood treated with iron sulphate to turn it grey.

MEDULLARY RAY FIGURING
Effect created by the medullary rays which radiate from the pith of the tree trunk. They produce the characteristic figure in quarter-sawn boards of oak and beech.

PATINA
Gloss and minor blemishes which woodwork acquires after years of polishing and use.

POLISHER'S MOP
A brush, often made from zorino, goat or squirrel hair used for application of polishes and also to access awkward areas.

ROSIN
A natural gum arising from the distillation of pure turpentine from pine trees. Available in coarse powder or lumps, it is an ingredient in beaumontage.

SLURRY
The paste formed when using plaster of Paris and water to make grainfiller.

STOCKINETTE
Also known as mutton cloth, a stretchy machine-knitted cloth used for burnishing.

STOPPER
A flexible material used for filling holes and creacks in wood (see 'beaumontage').

SUBSTRATE
A surface to which a finish is applied.

TEREBENE
A poisonous light yellow liquid used as a drier in oil polishing, and in the making of some revivers.

INCHES TO MILLIMETRES AND CENTIMETRES

mm = millimetres   cm = centimetres

inches	mm	cm	inches	cm	inches	cm
1/8	3	0.3	9	22.9	30	76.2
1/4	6	0.6	10	25.4	31	78.7
3/8	10	1.0	11	27.9	32	81.3
1/2	13	1.3	12	30.5	33	83.8
5/8	16	1.6	13	33.0	34	86.4
3/4	19	1.9	14	35.6	35	88.9
7/8	22	2.2	15	38.1	36	91.4
1	25	2.5	16	40.6	37	94.0
1 1/4	32	3.2	17	43.2	38	96.5
1 1/2	38	3.8	18	45.7	39	99.1
1 3/4	44	4.4	19	48.3	40	101.6
2	51	5.1	20	50.8	41	104.1
2 1/2	64	6.4	21	53.3	42	106.7
3	76	7.6	22	55.9	43	109.2
3 1/2	89	8.9	23	58.4	44	111.8
4	102	10.2	24	61.0	45	114.3
4 1/2	114	11.4	25	63.5	46	116.8
5	127	12.7	26	66.0	47	119.4
6	152	15.2	27	68.6	48	121.9
7	178	17.8	28	71.1	49	124.5
8	203	20.3	29	73.7	50	127.0

ABOUT THE AUTHOR

Ian Hosker began learning his craft at the age of 14 from his grandfather, whose range of skills seemed at that time to be awesome. Ian's initial adolescent curiosity rapidly became a passion as his skills and knowledge grew, a phenomenon that many workers with wood will be familiar with. The channel for this new-found passion became a business in furniture restoration and cabinetmaking, which ran alongside a career in mainstream education.

His clients have included interior designers (some with very distinguished clients themselves, offering the opportunity to work on some very fine pieces), and he has undertaken numerous private commissions.

Ian now lives in Devon with his wife Barbara and their two children, where he writes, teaches and demonstrates extensively on the subject of furniture – its history, construction and repair.

INDEX

TITLES AVAILABLE FROM
GMC PUBLICATIONS

BOOKS

Woodworking Plans and Projects . . . . .GMC Publications
40 More Woodworking Plans and Projects . . . . .GMC Publications
Woodworking Crafts Annual . . . . .GMC Publications
Woodworkers' Career & Educational Source Book .GMC Publications
Woodturning Techniques . . . . .GMC Publications
Useful Woodturning Projects . . . . .GMC Publications
Practical Tips for Woodturners . . . . .GMC Publications
Practical Tips for Turners and Carvers . . . . .GMC Publications
Green Woodwork . . . . .Mike Abbott
Easy to Make Dolls' House Accessories . . . . .Andrea Barham
Making Little Boxes from Wood . . . . .John Bennett
Woodturning Masterclass . . . . .Tony Boase
Furniture Restoration and Repair for Beginners . . . . .Kevin Jan Bonner
Woodturning Jewellery . . . . .Hilary Bowen
The Incredible Router . . . . .Jeremy Broun
Electric Woodwork . . . . .Jeremy Broun
Woodcarving: A Complete Course . . . . .Ron Butterfield
Making Fine Furniture: Projects . . . . .Tom Darby
Restoring Rocking Horses . . . . .Clive Green & Anthony Dew
Heraldic Miniature Knights . . . . .Peter Greenhill
Make Your Own Dolls' House Furniture . . . . .Maurice Harper
Practical Crafts: Seat Weaving . . . . .Ricky Holdstock
Multi-centre Woodturning . . . . .Ray Hopper
Complete Woodfinishing . . . . .Ian Hosker
Woodturning: A Source Book of Shapes . . . . .John Hunnex
Making Shaker Furniture . . . . .Barry Jackson
Upholstery: A Complete Course . . . . .David James
Upholstery Techniques and Projects . . . . .David James
The Upholsterer's Pocket Reference Book . . . . .David James
Designing and Making Wooden Toys . . . . .Terry Kelly
Making Dolls' House Furniture . . . . .Patricia King
Making Victorian Dolls' House Furniture . . . . .Patricia King
Making and Modifying Woodworking Tools . . . . .Jim Kingshott
The Workshop . . . . .Jim Kingshott
Sharpening: The Complete Guide . . . . .Jim Kingshott
Turning Wooden Toys . . . . .Terry Lawrence
Making Board, Peg and Dice Games . . . . .Jeff & Jennie Loader
Making Wooden Toys and Games . . . . .Jeff & Jennie Loader
Bert Marsh: Woodturner . . . . .Bert Marsh
The Complete Dolls' House Book . . . . .Jean Nisbett
The Secrets of the Dolls' House Makers . . . . .Jean Nisbett
Wildfowl Carving, Volume 1 . . . . .Jim Pearce
Make Money from Woodturning . . . . .Ann & Bob Phillips

VIDEOS

*GMC Publications regularly produces new books and videos
on a wide range of woodworking and craft subjects, and an increasing number of specialist
magazines, all available on subscription:*

MAGAZINES

WOODCARVING   WOODTURNING   BUSINESSMATTERS

All the publications are available through bookshops and newsagents,
or may be ordered by post from the publishers at:

**Castle Place, 166 High Street, Lewes, East Sussex, BN7 1XU.
Telephone (01273) 477374. Fax (01273) 477606.**

Credit Cards are accepted

PLEASE WRITE OR PHONE FOR A FREE CATALOGUE